CONTENTS

"YOU CHANGED CLOTHES? DAMN YOU, USUI! HOW DARE YOU ...AND WITH MY DAUGHTER!" KARIN THREW HERSELF IN FRONT OF HER FA-THER, DESPERATELY TRYING TO STOP HIM FROM STRANGLING KENTA.

4

STORY BY TOHRU KAI
ART BY YUNA KAGESAKI

HAMBURG // LONDON // LOS ANGELES // TOKYO

Chibi Vampire: The Novel 4
Written by Tohru Kai
Art by Yuna Kagesaki

Translation - Andrew Cunningham
English Adaptation - Ethan Russell
Design and Layout - Carolyn Wendt
Cover Design - Colin Graham
Senior Editor - Jenna Winterberg

Editor - Kara Stambach
Pre-Production Supervisor - Erika Terriquez
Digital Imaging Manager - Chris Buford
Creative Director - Anne Marie Horne
Production Manager - Elisabeth Brizzi
Managing Editor - Vy Nguyen
Editor-in-Chief - Rob Tokar
Publisher - Mike Kiley
President and C.O.O. - John Parker
C.E.O. and Chief Creative Officer - Stuart Levy

A **TOKYOPOP** Novel

TOKYOPOP Inc.
5900 Wilshire Blvd. Suite 2000
Los Angeles, CA 90036

E-mail: info@TOKYOPOP.com
Come visit us online at www.TOKYOPOP.com

ISBN: 978-1-59816-925-6

First TOKYOPOP printing: January 2008
10 9 8 7 6 5 4 3 2 1
Printed in the USA

"UGH, YOU REEK OF GARLIC! STAY AWAY!" ANJU'S DOLL BOOGIE BARKED AT KARIN THE MOMENT SHE GOT HOME FROM WORK.

. . . . .

"YOU MADE MY DAUGHTER CRY?" KARIN LOOKED UP IN SURPRISE AT THE SOUND OF HER FATHER'S VOICE.

Hey! Kijima . . ."

Kijima Hidemi opened his eyes to discover his head was nestled in his arms. *Whoops!* Hidemi realized he had fallen asleep during yet another meeting.

One of the fifth grade teachers had woken him with a stern hiss and now glared at him through officious glasses.

Hidemi nodded a silent thanks as he glanced at his watch. He'd been asleep for only a few minutes.

The students had gone home after a half day, leaving the teachers and school officials to suffer through a staff meeting. The leader of the meeting droned on: "We still need to find a budget for security, but the students will begin moaning soon if we don't manage to get the pool open."

There had been a big fuss about a peeping Tom at a nearby swimming pool; however, no arrests had been made. The Aoba Elementary pool usually was open to students during summer vacation, provided there was a teacher there to watch over the children. With the rise in disturbing incidents, though, they were reconsidering allowing the children to use the pool. Both sides had put forward heated arguments, but a formal decision was on hold until after a school board inspection.

As the attendees filed out after the meeting, Hidemi called out to the teacher who had awoken him: "Thanks again, Makihara." Hidemi and Makihara were around the same age and so tended to look out for each other among the spinsters and geriatric eccentrics who taught at Aoba Elementary.

"No problem," Makihara replied. "Consider it payback for covering my lifeguard duty. Did the little monsters wear you out?"

"You had a funeral to attend," Hidemi pointed out. "The kids are fine. What's wearing me out is trying to find another job once the term ends. This was a temporary assignment for me." Hidemi was filling in for a teacher who was recovering from a broken leg, and his gig ended in September.

"I'm sure you'll find something soon enough. The kids all love you. My kids got excited when they heard we'd be teaching that group class together."

With that comment, Hidemi's thoughts turned to one specific girl in Makihara's class. Her parents were naturalized citizens, as evidenced by her dramatic platinum blonde hair. She almost never spoke, but she seemed more aloof than shy. Her delicate, doll-like features had earned her a number of passionate fans among the boys in class—and an equal number of enemies among the girls.

Makihara's not blind, Hidemi thought. *He must have noticed. Maybe I'm wrong. I observed her only during our shared teaching group. All the same, I'm leaving in September—and bullying requires swift action. It's worth mentioning.*

"Not to change the subject, but in your class—"

A collision distracted Hidemi before he could complete his thought: *there's a girl called Anju Maaka.*

A female teacher had tried to slide around Hidemi, but she wound up walking directly into him instead. "Kijima! If you must talk in the hall, be careful where you walk!" Hidemi knew her as second grade teacher Tsujikawa Shizuka. She loomed imperiously, aided by towering high heels.

"Sorry. No need to get so—"

"You have some nerve telling me off after you fell asleep in the meeting," Shizuka snapped. Her eyes seemed to whittle him down from behind her heavy black spectacles. "You're in charge of children. Shape up! You may be nothing more than a substitute, but you still can make a big impact on your students. Look at the way you dress! You shouldn't wear a T-shirt on inspection day."

Hidemi looked down at the T-shirt peeking out from the top button of his dress shirt. He was merely a necktie short of matching Makihara; neither man, however, could compare to Shizuka herself. The prim teacher wore a heavy navy suit despite the summer heat.

"Now, if you'll excuse me . . ." Shizuka whirled on one foot and clicked her way down the hall, unwilling to expend the energy to finish her sentence.

Hidemi watched her go with annoyance. After all, she was in only her second year of teaching, and all three of them were more or less the same age.

"I can't believe *she's* roaming the halls!"

"Calm down, Hidemi. I know Tsujikawa rides you, but—"

"'But' nothing. She really rubs me the wrong way. I can't stand women like her."

"I'm sure it's stress about the inspection," Makihara said diplomatically. "I've heard bad things about the current board."

"Like what?

Makihara looked around furtively, lowering his voice to a whisper. "I haven't seen anything myself, but the principal said Kuramochi is letting things slip through the cracks and Fuchi keeps forgetting things. Meanwhile, chairman Nunoura has been criticizing the tiniest things since his divorce."

"The principal's quite a gossip."

Makihara dropped his voice another notch. "That's not all. One of them collects pictures of little girls. They found an album full of pictures of girls in strange outfits."

"What? And he's on the Board of Education?"

"Shhh!"

Hidemi clamped a hand over his mouth. He understood where Makihara was going with his story. Following direction from people you couldn't trust was terrifying. This inspection was going to be a major headache.

That puts Tsujikawa in the same boat as the rest of us. The inspection can't be making her that prickly, though. It must be something personal. Hidemi felt himself getting irritated again. *These arrogant women are everywhere I go! My mother, sister, aunt, and grandmother all went on about how I should quit being a teacher when I was back home for the Bon Festival. Then, I get back here and Tsujikawa has it in for me. They're killing me! What did I ever do to them?*

The least he could do was have someone nice in his private life. *If only I could meet someone cute and quiet—a relaxing girl . . .*

Hidemi gave a long, deep sigh.

The summer sun was shining relentlessly, yet the town square was filled with couples and families intent on ignoring the heat.

The Aiai Festival had begun as a simple flea market; as it had grown more famous, advertising, performances, and market stalls had been added. Held every August, it now had become the biggest event in Higashinomori.

A gentle breeze rustled through the square, carrying the smell of flour and oil. The tantalizing hint of garlic and meat hid behind the aroma, whetting appetites left and right.

"Gyoza! Five hundred yen per pack! Free samples!" Karin Maaka held out a tray with samples for passersby. She wore a traditional Chinese dress, despite offering gyoza.

"Chuka Banpaku is now open in Amusement Square!" She wiped her brow during a lull in customer activity. Although the heat was nearly unbearable, she thought, *I can't stop now! This job pays one hundred yen more an hour than usual!*

Karin had taken on a second job earlier in the summer, handing out samples of gyoza at an indoor theme park. Today, she had been sent to the festival to help advertise the shop instead.

Two cooks were frying gyoza as quickly as possible in the stall behind her. Karin knew they were having a worse time of it than she was.

"Free samples! Come to Chuka Banpaku in Amusement Square for more!"

"Karin?" A familiar voice made her jump.

"Kenta!"

Karin felt her body temperature flutter two degrees at the sight of her classmate. The Chinese dress she wore had a long slit up one leg and drew a lot of attention to her chest. She would have preferred not to be seen in it by anyone she knew—especially not Kenta Usui.

"Working here today?"

"Um, yeah! You too?" Karin said, relieved that he hadn't made fun of her outfit.

"Yep. People buy a lot here at the market and have it shipped home."

Karin noticed Kenta was wearing his Black Dog Damien Delivery Company uniform.

"Anyway, good luck," he said.

"Wait!" Karin held out her tray. "Take a sample."

A smile spread across Kenta's normally intimidating features. Chronic poverty left him perpetually hungry.

"Thanks!" He picked up a single gyoza and disappeared into the crowd. Karin admired his

manners—anyone else would have grabbed two or three. Her heart beat quickly and she felt a familiar sensation well up inside her.

Is Kenta getting enough to eat? I hope he isn't working too hard. . . .

School started in two more weeks, and Karin would be able to resume bringing him lunch each day. She resolved to think of some healthy meals to cook for him.

"Maaka! New batch!" one of the cooks called out. "You drifted off there for a moment. Thinking about your boyfriend?"

"No way!" she wailed. She grabbed the new tray and darted back into the crowd before the cook could draw her out.

We're not like that! Karin fumed internally. *Kenta is just a friend! He keeps my secret and I bring him lunch! That's all! Why does everyone think he's my boyfriend?*

Karin and the rest of the Maaka clan were vampires, descendants of a family that had migrated to Japan two hundred years prior.

Kenta had moved into an apartment near Karin's house in April, transferring into her class and also winding up with a part-time job at the same family restaurant where she worked. With that much overlap in their routine, it hadn't taken Kenta long to figure out Karin's secret. He never had accused her of being a monster; instead, he'd agreed to help Karin avoid exposing the truth to anyone else. So, once she found out about his dire economic situation, Karin began bringing lunches to him at school by way of thanks.

Kenta is just a friend, she repeated to herself. Then, she turned her attention back to her job: "Who wants some gyoza? Chuka Banpaku, open now at Amusement Square!"

The festival ended at six, and Karin planned on heading directly home without making a trip back to the main shop. Like all her plans, however, this one was unlikely to come to fruition. . . .

It was half past six by the time Karin had finished helping the cooks load everything into the van. She changed her clothes in the bathroom of City Hall and headed for the station. By the time she squeezed onto a train, it was nearly seven: rush hour.

Karin rarely rode trains and found the crowd suffocating. She was buried between much taller adults and fought to gulp mouthfuls of air. She forced her way through the crowd toward the marginally less-packed area away from the doors. When the train slowed, the shifting crowd at her back pushed her into a newly empty seat.

Phew! I can breathe here. Karin rested her bag on her knees and piled her elbows on top. Even seated, it was hardly a relaxing ride. The car swayed wildly at every turn, causing the businessman seated next to her to brush against her chest.

No way!

The businessman had his arms folded innocuously; however, the crook of his elbow hid an open hand, which squeezed Karin's breast at each turn. At first, she had chalked up the unwanted advance as an accident; then, with each turn of the track, he resumed "accidentally" squeezing and stroking.

Although Karin had heard of casual molestation on the trains, it hadn't ever happened to her. She wanted to scream, yet she was too petrified to move. And the assault was humiliating enough without the added embarrassment of shouting in a crowd. She crossed her own arms in an attempt to shield herself.

The businessman was nonplussed: He subtly pushed her hand aside and touched her again.

Stop! Somebody help!

Embarrassment and horror made her tear up. Karin looked around herself, searching for help. Her eyes met those of a young man, who blinked back at her.

The train braked suddenly, sending the standing passengers flying forward with inertia. The movement tossed Karin into her molester. A wave of horror washed over her.

"What the hell do you think you're doing?" a voice shouted angrily. It was the man Karin had made eye contact with moments before. He grabbed the businessman's arm and hauled him away from Karin.

"What do you mean?" the businessman protested lamely.

"I'm the one asking you! The back of your hand might be an accident, but you were grabbing this girl with your palm! Molesting a child right in front of me! She's crying now! I got a good look at what you were up to when the train braked, you filthy pervert! Aren't you a little old to be this stupid?"

The newcomer raged with a fire that belied his small frame. After unleashing this torrent of abuse, he turned and glanced down at Karin. "You guys weren't role playing or anything, were you?"

"No way! I've never seen this creep before!" Karin wailed.

The train stopped. The molester shook himself free of the smaller man's grip and pushed his way through the crowd to reach the freshly opened doors.

The newcomer threw himself into the empty seat next to Karin.

"I'm sorry. I should have had a better grip on him."

"Forget about it." Karin shook her head. Her heart was still beating furiously. She invested a lot of time and energy into blending in, wary of attracting attention lest her true nature be discovered. She never could have gone to the police. Having someone scare off the molester without involving the law was something of a relief.

"Anyway, are you okay?" she asked.

"I'm fine. I should be the one asking if you're okay."

Her savior grinned, white teeth gleaming against caramel skin. He looked a little younger than Karin's brother Ren—nineteen or twenty, Karin surmised. He wore jeans and a T-shirt, with the latter partially hidden behind a zipped vest.

"I could tell you were uncomfortable, but I couldn't see his hands. I thought maybe you had to pee or something."

"No!" Karin gasped.

"I know, I know. I just didn't know *then*. I was going to say something to you the moment you sat down; then, I thought I might embarrass you. I should have called out right away."

"Huh?" Karin looked at him in surprise. It sounded like he knew her.

"You're friends with Anju Maaka, aren't you?"

Karin gaped at him, not expecting that name in a million years.

The newcomer tilted his head, puzzled. "You don't know her? I'm sure I've seen you with her. I think her parents immigrated over here; she has a Japanese name, but she looks like a little French doll—silver hair and eyes like green tea. You'd know her if you saw her. She wears a lot of frilly Goth clothes and always carries a weird doll around . . . very pretty, but standoffish."

"I know Anju," Karin said.

"Thought so. I was sure I'd seen you walking together. Friends?"

"No. I'm her sister. Karin . . ."

"Seriously? You look nothing like her!"

Karin hung her head. His exclamation of disbelief had come right after a lengthy spiel about her little sister's incredibly beautiful, doll-like features. Anyone would be depressed by a direct comparison. Embarrassed by her own dejection, Karin felt herself turning red.

The man quickly realized his blunder. "Ah! Sorry. I really didn't mean that as a reflection on you. I mean, she may be pretty, but you're cute. No guy would ever say a cute girl was any worse than a pretty one. Pretty girls make a tingle run down your spine, whereas the cute ones make your heart skip a beat. No, seriously. Pretty girls all eat weird food designed only for them. Takoyaki? Okonomiyaki? Yakiniku? Never. And no way am I eating French food."

The speech had veered so wildly off course that Karin couldn't help but laugh.

"See? Girls like you always should be laughing. I know you agree. Um. What was I talking about?"

"Anju."

Karin wondered how he knew her little sister.

The man seemed to pick up on her thought and awkwardly scratched his head. "Right. I should have said before: I'm a teacher at her elementary school."

"You're kidding! I thought you were in college!" Karin was genuinely surprised.

"Ouch!" he grimaced. "I'm short, too."

The newcomer introduced himself as Hidemi Kijima.

"I'm twenty-three," he explained. "This is my second year of teaching. Of course, I can't find a decent job, so I'm working as a substitute—one school after another. One of the teachers at Aoba Elementary is out with an injury, so I'm teaching fourth grade there until the end of September."

"So, you aren't Anju's teacher, then. She's in fifth grade." Karin blanched at the thought of Anju attracting attention from anyone other than her teacher. Her distinct appearance and frequent absences from school brought with them the threat of exposure for the family.

Although Karin was a defective vampire, the rest of the Maaka clan boasted the traditional characteristics, including a fear of sunlight. Only Anju could venture out in the day like Karin; in her case, it was because she was too young for her vampire nature to take dominance, though—her natural inclinations mirrored those of the rest of the family. Anju went to school solely on overcast days and usually stayed up all night. Their parents never attended parent-teacher nights or extracurricular activities.

Strange children, strange parents. People are bound to notice eventually. Karin started to get anxious.

Hidemi regarded her gravely. "You get along with your sister, right, despite being older? What are you, a high school student?"

"Freshman," Karin confirmed. "Four years older. And we do *not* get along."

Karin hung her head, ashamed at how often Anju had to bail her out of trouble.

Hidemi didn't seem to notice Karin's reaction, though. "Good. I'm glad she has a sister. Anju seems a little out of the loop at school. I don't think she's being bullied or anything . . . still, she seems isolated— especially from the girls."

Hidemi first became aware of the problem at the end of June, when the older students had gathered in the gym for a group class. Two boys and two girls from the fourth, fifth, and sixth grades had formed a special unit, but the fifth grade group had taken an especially long time to get organized . . . because none of the girls had wanted to partner with Anju.

When the boys noticed this, they all tried to get Anju to join their teams, ignoring the rules about how many of each gender they were supposed to have. Some of the girls began jeering in response, and Hidemi had to step in eventually.

The fifth grade had fewer girls than boys, so they wound up putting Anju in a group with three guys.

"Anju didn't seem to care about any of it," Hidemi explained. "It's been bugging me, though. I thought she might be repressing her emotions or something. . . . Does she talk at home?"

"She's never been very talkative," Karin admitted. "I mean, she talks a lot if she's interested in something." Little interested Anju, however, beyond her collection of dolls. Karin found them absolutely terrifying and tried to avoid the subject whenever possible.

"I was worried," Hidemi continued. "She's not in my class, though, so I rarely see her. And now that the semester's over . . . I mean, the pool's open during the summer, but Anju never comes there. Not surprising, really—she doesn't seem to like sunlight."

Karin stiffened. Not liking sunlight was a clear sign of vampirism. *Has he figured it out? Is he trying to trick me into admitting it?*

Her heart began beating faster. Karin fretted about whether to speak or keep silent. Which was stranger? Giving a weird response definitely would make things worse.

"Maybe she has a hypersensitivity to ultraviolet light? She could be one of those people who breaks out in hives in the sun—maybe that's why she always wears long sleeves, even in summer. She doesn't seem to eat much, either. It could be allergies. That's hard on a kid."

Karin was so relieved that she almost slid out of her seat. *If Anju didn't eat something, it probably had garlic in it. Thank goodness he didn't notice.*

Although she relaxed, her heart pumped faster. *Huh? Why is my heart beating so quickly if there's nothing wrong? Oh, no! My blood rush! Not now! I just injected someone!*

With anxiety over the molester and Anju keeping her preoccupied, she hadn't noticed the warm flush on her cheeks or her pounding heart. It was strictly a biological response, for Karin was a very unusual vampire. Normal vampires grow hungry in the presence of humans with their favorite blood type. For Karin, however, the situation was reversed: Her heart produce dexcess blood—too much for her to contain. It was an instinctive reaction, one she couldn't control. When the blood reached a certain limit, she would have to bite someone and pump the excess into that other person.

Most vampires were bloodsuckers; she was a blood-injector. And the quality that triggered her instinct was unhappiness.

Karin glanced at the man next to her. Now that she had noticed her blood rush, she could tell: There was an aura of unhappiness all around Hidemi, and this was why her blood was rushing.

Oh, no! He's much too close to me! He isn't that unhappy, though, so it isn't bad yet. . . .

Usually, it was Kenta who set her off. Every time he got close to her, her blood would surge. His unhappiness had led directly to his discovery of her true nature.

Kenta keeps it a secret. I nearly did something awful to him the other day, and he wasn't angry at all. Augh! Karin grew so embarrassed by the memory that she nearly ran away. She shook her head to clear the memories.

"Anju doesn't have allergies?"

"Sorry, I was shaking my head about something else. Yep! She has a ton of allergies!" Karin had been so flustered by the blood rush that she'd forgotten she was in the middle of a conversation.

Hidemi seemed moderately unhappy to Karin, and her blood was increasing at a reasonable rate. *I'm fine! I can handle this. I just need to stay calm. As long as I don't panic . . . don't think about it too much!*

She had injected someone with blood two or three days ago and therefore was in no immediate danger. When she went too long without letting off steam, Karin would suffer explosive nosebleeds. She reckoned she would be fine as long as she focused on the discussion.

"Anyway, I thought I would make sure she wasn't being bullied," Hidemi was saying. "When I saw you, I thought maybe I should talk to you about it. We teachers can keep an eye out at school, but you should talk with her at home, Karin."

Anju was unlikely to take that well. It was usually Karin who went to Anju for help and advice, not the other way around. Karin's life was a series of blunders, whereas Anju was older than her years and much more in control. Karin never saw her little sister panic or cry. She couldn't imagine Anju much cared what the other girls thought of her.

Her best friend is a doll with the soul of a serial killer trapped inside, Karin thought. All the same, she was glad people were keeping an eye out for her sister. Hidemi seemed like a good teacher despite his youth. *And he saved me from a molester, so he's obviously a good guy!*

The loudspeaker announced the name of an approaching station as the train slowed.

Hidemi adjusted the backpack on his lap. "I get off here," he said.

"Me too . . ."

The train stopped and the doors opened. A wave of passengers spilled out of the car, Karin and Hidemi among them.

"I take the number two bus from here. What about you?" he asked.

Standing next to him like this, Karin realized how short he was. Hidemi had a light frame and a baby face that made it easy to talk to him.

"There's a bus, but it doesn't come often," Karin said. "My house isn't that far away. I usually walk."

"Shall I come with you?"

"I'm fine. It's still early." It would never do for a human to discover the location of a vampire's lair. Karin also was worried about the steady urgency growing inside her. She wanted to get away as quickly as possible to avoid a situation.

Sunset came earlier each day as August wore on, and the sky already was a deep blue by the time Karin left the station. She could see the faint shimmer of stars forming.

"Goodbye! And thank you for saving me, Kijima-sensei," she said, unsure of how to address him.

"'Sensei'? I feel like I'm still at work!"

"You teach at Anju's school . . ."

"I know, I know. I'm the one who started that conversation. Anyway, keep an eye on your sister for me, will you?"

Karin nodded. Suddenly, someone tapped her on the shoulder.

"Excuse me, ma'am? I'm lost!"

Karin turned around, surprised by a thick accent. She saw a tall foreign man looming over her.

"Where is Jori Hall? I'm in a hurry. The concert is about to start!"

The stranger wore a long black coat and a formal hat despite the August heat—presumably for the concert. His voice was so loud it hurt her ears. She took a step backward, pulling away from the hand on her shoulder.

"I'm sorry, I don't know."

Karin's body suddenly shook, and she almost screamed. It was as if an invisible hand was squeezing her heart. A sharp pain spread from her chest all the way up behind her nose, every blood vessel in her body shuddering.

My blood rush? It's so strong! She glanced at Hidemi behind her. The teacher gave off an aura of unhappiness far stronger than he had before. The feeling almost stabbed into her skin.

The dark stranger followed her glance. "Do you know where it is, boy?" he asked.

"Who's a 'boy'?" Hidemi retorted. He made a wounded gesture toward the train station. "I don't know where it is. Ask the police."

The interloper walked briskly toward the station. Karin's blood rush ebbed slightly as Hidemi's unhappiness dimmed. The teacher still scowled, nonetheless, one hand pressed to his temple.

"Is something wrong?" Karin asked.

"Oh," he shook himself to snap out of it. "Sorry. Sudden headache."

"Are you okay? You look pale."

"It's nothing. I'll get over it." Hidemi tried to grin, which made him look worse.

Karin pointed at a row of shops opposite the station. "You look awful. There's a drugstore over there. Maybe you should take something."

Hidemi blinked at her, surprised. Then, a soft shine spread across his eyes. "You're so nice! Thank you. You really don't have to worry, though. It's a psychological reaction—to that black coat. Ever since I was a child, old suits like that have given me chills. Maybe I was attacked by a vampire or something."

This obviously was supposed to be a joke; still, Karin could feel the blood draining from her face. For a moment, she wondered if Hidemi really had been bitten by a vampire. The creature would have erased his memories, leaving only a fear of black coats in its place.

"No need to look so scared! I was joking," Hidemi said, scratching his cheek.

Karin realized that she had taken a step back, and she quickly shook her head. "No, I know that. . . ."

She knew it wasn't likely. There simply weren't that many vampires around.

Hidemi took his hand off his head.

A bus slowly pulled into the hub.

"That's my bus," Hidemi said. "So, I guess . . . make sure you don't get molested again on the way home. Do you have a noisemaker or anything with you? You should keep it in your hand, not your bag. Anyway, see you around."

"Sure. Thanks!"

Karin waved, and Hidemi flashed the same cheery smile he'd had on board the train before darting toward his bus.

Karin took a deep breath and began the short walk to her house. Her blood rush had subsided at last, to her relief. The respite gave her a chance to think things over.

Why did Hidemi trigger my blood rush? He seems so cheerful. And why does he hate black coats so much? He seems like such a good person. He was really worried about Anju, and he saved me from that molester—who could've had a knife! Too scary!

She shivered, her imagination getting the best of her.

The news was filled with stories of thieves stabbing the people who caught them. Karin had been too embarrassed to scream, but she figured the people on the train would have been too afraid to help if she had.

Thank goodness Kijima-sensei was there. He was so easy to talk to.

Hidemi was eight years older than Karin; his baby face made him seem just within reach, though. His cheery attitude and casual manner had put her at ease even though she had been molested. Karin never had been very good around men, yet she'd managed to talk to him without much difficulty.

Kenta was the only other male not in her family that she'd spoken to as easily. He was much taller than her, so much so that looking up at him during a conversation of any length made her neck hurt. He usually looked frightening enough that he could drive off a thug with a single glance. Yet, in reality, he was the nicest person Karin ever had met.

The more she thought about him, the hotter her face grew.

Oh, no! Karin thought. *My face is turning red. It's like thinking about him makes me blush!* Karin put her hands on her cheeks. Nobody was looking at her. She was embarrassed anyway.

I'd better get home! I have summer school homework, and then I work again tomorrow. . . .

"Here you are: one garlic steak set." The next day was sunny again, making the tabletop where Karin put the plate down glow. She caught a glimpse of movement out of the corner of her eye and turned to see Kenta hurrying down the hall from the staff room. He had arranged his schedule very tightly and so was almost always late for work.

Karin was off in another half hour. It wasn't a lot of time to spend working together, but Karin didn't want Kenta to bring up what had happened the other day if business lulled. The thought terrified her.

A few days earlier, when Karin's blood rush had reached its peak capacity, she'd lost control and threw herself on Kenta in hopes of injecting him for relief. Despite his being a classmate and a coworker, she had lunged for him anyway. She remembered pressing her body against his, her lips parted and hovering over his throat. She couldn't recall if they had touched skin.

So embarrassing!

Karin had forced herself to stop at the last minute, exploding with blood from her nose and mouth. She soon passed out. She vaguely recalled the sensation of something warm tightly embracing her. When she awoke, Kenta revealed he had been taking care of her the whole time.

Had the embrace been Kenta's arms? There was no way she could ask him to find out for sure. *No way am I asking him about that! Knocking him down and trying to bite him is one thing; if I ended up hugging him, though . . . there's no excuse! It's too embarrassing!*

Her head was so hot it felt like it was on fire. Karin wrapped her arms around her head and swayed from side to side.

"What are you doing, Karin?"

She looked up to find Kenta staring down at her.

"Are you coming down with something?" he inquired.

"No! It's nothing!" Karin realized she was still standing in the middle of the restaurant. Flustered, she noticed a customer standing up in a bid to catch her attention. "Um. I have to ring up this customer!" Karin ran toward the cash register.

Gah! This is so embarrassing! What does he really think about what happened the other day? I know he said he hates the way I always run away instead of talking. . . . Did that refer only to trying to bite

35

him—or did it include hugging, as well? Karin was none the wiser.

She cashed out the customer through sheer force of habit, her brain entirely focused on Kenta.

He doesn't seem angry, but he might be sick and tired of my messes.

Still behind the register, she hung her head. Then, she heard the automatic doors sliding open and reflexively looked up to greet the new diner.

"Welcome to Julian . . ."

Karin's voice trailed off. The man coming into the restaurant was the same man who had saved her from the molester the day before. Hidemi stood in the doorway with a jacket under one arm, wiping sweat from his forehead with a handkerchief in the other. His eyes flared when he saw Karin.

"Oh, Karin! You work here?"

"Yes." Karin bowed. "Thank you for yesterday."

"Ha! Forget about it. You can't thank me forever. You got home okay last night? No other strange guys after you?"

"Nothing like that," she said vaguely. Her mind was preoccupied with getting a read on the unhappiness Hidemi radiated. She barely could feel it today. It was as faint as it had been on the train the day before.

Hidemi tugged on his tie, assuming there was another reason for Karin's hesitation.

"The suit looks weird on me, huh?"

Karin knew it was impolite to agree; all the same, with his baby face, Hidemi looked like he was headed for the *Shichi-go-san* festival.

"Not at all," she stammered.

"Seriously, I don't mind at all. I completely agree. I'm on my way back from a job interview, though. You can't wear jeans and a T-shirt to meet the director of a private school, can you? Not if you actually want the job!"

"You're job hunting? Oh right, you said you would finish at Aoba Elementary in September."

"Yep. Need to find something to do after that. Nothing's a lock yet, but it looks as if I may be at a private elementary school in the fall."

"Well, I'm glad you found something," Karin said, grinning. He seemed so happy.

"Sir, this seat's ready," a voice called out behind them. Kenta had finished busing a table and was now ready to seat Hidemi.

Kenta . . . A dull pain spread through Karin's heart.

"Whoops! Can't distract you from work. See you later, Karin," Hidemi said, heading toward the table.

Karin looked around, but nobody else needed to be cashed out. As she left the register, she saw Kenta heading toward the kitchen with a pile of dirty plates.

Kenta saw us talking. What should I do? It wasn't like they had done anything wrong. Karin simply had thanked Hidemi for saving her, and they had talked about job hunting. The thought of Kenta seeing her flirting with another man made it hard to breathe, though.

Kenta's just a friend! Karin thought, furious. *I don't think of him as anything else!*

"Hey, Karin!"

"What?" Karin snapped out of her daze at the sound of Kenta's voice.

He handed her a tray with a glass of water on it and pointed to Hidemi's table.

"You know him, right? I thought you should be the one to serve him. Business is slow right now, so you can chat with him a little without getting in trouble."

Karin couldn't tell from his blank expression what Kenta was driving at. Was it a helpful gesture or something sarcastic? Karin knew Kenta wouldn't need to resort to sarcasm about Hidemi. They were just friends, after all. Even so, she was rattled. "Know him? I don't really . . ."

"You'd better hurry. He's looking at us."

Karin glanced toward the seat and met Hidemi's gaze. Hidemi flashed his teeth and waved.

Kenta put the tray in Karin's hands and headed back to the kitchen.

Hidemi spurs my blood rush. That goes for Kenta as well, though. I'm just taking his order, not sitting down next to him like I did yesterday. I should be fine.

Still a little nervous, Karin carried the glass to Hidemi's table.

"Thanks," he said in a low voice. "Are they upset with you or something?"

"Huh?"

Hidemi glanced meaningfully at Kenta. "That guy was scolding you, right? He glared at you."

"No!" Karin fought to suppress a giggle. Kenta had narrow, beady eyes, and people often thought he looked angry. "He always looks like that."

"Oh. I thought I'd gotten you into trouble. I was going to apologize."

Karin smiled. "I'm fine. He was saying I should take your order, because I know you and we aren't very busy right now. By the way, I haven't had the chance to talk to my sister yet. Sorry."

Anju had been out practicing with her bats when Karin had arrived home the night before. Her sister was nearly nocturnal, and Karin had given up waiting and went to sleep without seeing her.

"Nothing to apologize for. I know it's a delicate matter. Hard to get started, right?"

"Um . . ."

"I know we should be taking care of things at school first; thanks for agreeing to talk to her, anyway. I'm glad she has you to look after her. You're a good sister."

Karin flushed. "It's all because of you."

She knew Anju probably preferred to be isolated from the other students; at the same time, she admired the way Hidemi seemed concerned about her well-being. Anju wasn't even in his class, and Hidemi had said he was leaving the school at the end of the summer.

Karin bowed her head. "Thank you so much!"

"Stop that! It's my job, nothing worth bowing about!" Hidemi snapped, waving his hands around.

"Welcome to Julian!" The staff cried out in unison as the front door opened again. A new customer had entered.

"Welcome!" Karin called, glancing toward the door. Her eyes nearly popped out of her head.

A small group of diners had entered the diner, all wearing bizarre costumes. One was dressed in a kinky nurse's uniform, another in a science fiction outfit, and a third in shiny faux-military dress. Karin scarcely had time to assume they were dressed for the festival when a wave of unhappiness nearly knocked her over. Her entire body shook.

She spun around to find Hidemi staring at the newcomers, eyes wide with horror. One of the newcomers was dressed as a fantasy character in a black cape and hat. It was the least spectacular outfit of the group; its impact on Hidemi, however, was epic.

Hidemi fixated his gaze on the black uniform and became immobile. His unhappy aura sent Karin's pulse racing.

That cape must be as bad as a long black coat for Hidemi! Karin thought. Black clothing seemed to draw out his unhappiness. She watched as he pressed a hand to the side of his head, grimacing.

Karin covered the lower half of her face with her hands. She could feel heat swelling behind her nose.

Oh, no! This is the real thing! I have to get this man out of Hidemi's sight before I explode!

Karin reckoned this was the best solution for Hidemi, as well, given that merely looking at the diner gave him a headache. It was as if the teacher had seen something terrifying. His eyes darted around the man in the cape, who seemed rooted to the spot.

Karin pointed at the seat on the other side of the table.

"Um. Is your head hurting? Maybe you should sit over here . . . sensei."

"Oh, yeah." Hidemi quickly realizing what Karin was driving at. He switched chairs, turning his back to the cosplayers.

"Thanks. You've forgotten my name, haven't you?"

"Um . . ."

"No use hiding it! You called me 'sensei.'"

Karin turned a shade redder. She hadn't forgotten it completely. She knew it started with the letter 'K,' at least. *Kizaki? Kiyama?*

"Hidemi Kijima," he reminded her, ruefully. "Calling me 'sensei' makes me sound like a street vendor."

"Sorry!" Karin blurted.

"It's okay. There's no need to make such a fuss. Although you may have forgotten my name, you remembered about my headaches."

Karin couldn't tell Hidemi it was because they triggered her blood rush. She felt guilty about not remembering his name and resolved not to call him "sensei."

"I don't understand it myself," Hidemi said, referring to his headache. "I have no idea what happens to me. Fragments of lost memories flash before my eyes whenever I see black clothing: a woman screaming, the feeling of falling onto my shoulders, the smell of blood . . ."

"Blood?" Karin stiffened.

If blood were involved, whatever he was blocking couldn't be anything good. If Hidemi had fallen victim to some sort of crime, though, if he couldn't remember, the people who'd been around him still ought to.

The joke he'd made the night before floated through her mind. *Maybe he really was attacked by a vampire when his was a kid and had most of his memories of the encounter erased. . . . Maybe my father did it!*

Her heart nearly leapt out of her chest.

Karin's father always wore a long black coat when he went out to feed. The foreigner who had set off Hidemi the previous night had been about her father's size. Vampires usually left their victims alive, erasing their memories after the event to avoid drawing suspicion. Karin fought the feeling of panic, knowing her father never would target an innocent child.

Hidemi frowned when he saw how upset Karin was. He titled his head with concern.

"Is something wrong? You're waving your arms around—"

"No!" she squeaked. "Mr. Kijima, you grew up in Osaka, right?

If a vampire were at the root of his fears, it couldn't be her father: Osaka was well outside the Maaka clan's territory. It must have been some other vampire.

"No. I was born in Osaka, but I spent part of my childhood here. When I returned to Osaka, I already hated black coats. There were all sorts of problems during school plays, let me tell you. Something must have happened here, I guess. I don't remember a lot, honestly."

"Argh!"

Her hopes instantly dashed, Karin clutched her head. She was almost convinced her father was involved now.

"Not again!" Hidemi wailed. "Something's obviously wrong with you!"

"It's nothing! It's just my blood rush!"

"Your what?"

"Nothing! Um . . . I meant to ask if your headache was better, but my tongue got in the way!"

Hidemi smiled. "Much better, thank you."

"Good."

"I'm sorry, I still haven't ordered. Can I get the 'B' lunch set with rice and oolong tea? It isn't too late, is it?"

"Lunch runs until two, so you're in time. That's a 'B' lunch set with rice and oolong tea. Coming right up!"

The order taken, Karin turned to leave. She never heard Hidemi whisper to himself: "What a great girl . . ."

Instead, her eyes locked with Kenta's as her friend carried water over to the cosplay group's table. All her attention shifted instantly to him.

Kenta quickly averted his eyes, which left a sharp pain in Karin's chest.

Kenta saw me! Karin thought frantically. *Did he hear me blather about my blood rush?*

Had he been watching her in case she made a mistake, so he could help out? He seemed a little too grim for that. . . .

He's disgusted with me! All these mistakes . . . He may have covered for me so far, but if I accidentally tell someone what I am, how can he fix that? It's so embarrassing!

Hidemi's lunch was ready less than five minutes later. "Here you are! One 'B' lunch set!"

When she reached him, Karin realized the powerful unhappiness had faded away again. Turning his back to the man in the black cape had helped. Her own blood rush had stopped, as well. Karin put Hidemi's lunch in front of him, greatly relieved.

He grinned up at her. "Thanks. Say, I know this is a little sudden, but do you like amusement parks?"

"Sure." Karin paused for a moment. "Some of the rides are a little too scary, but most of them . . ."

The truth was that Karin adored amusement parks. She rarely could afford to go, though. Most roller coasters cost at least five hundred yen per ride. She had to work a full hour to earn that much, and it seemed a terrible waste to spend it on three minutes of fun.

"Are you free tomorrow?" Hidemi continued. "A friend of mine at the paper gave me some free tickets to Shiinoki Sky Land. Want to come? They're good until the end of the month, and I'm not going to use them otherwise."

"Tomorrow?"

This was a problem. Hidemi made her blood rush.

"Yeah. I thought I'd drag you along with me to make it more fun. I've been knocking myself out trying to find a job, and I could use a day off. If you have the time, will you come with me? I'll pay for everything, of course—to thank you for worrying about me. Or do you work tomorrow?"

"No, not tomorrow."

"Considering it's so hot, we could go to the water park, if you prefer."

"No!" Karin's face flushed with embarrassment. "No swimming for me!"

Karin actually liked swimming, but she wanted nothing to do with a boy seeing her in her swimsuit. She didn't mind at school, considering that everyone wore their school suits, but that didn't work at a public pool. She'd been swimming only with female friends. Even Kenta hadn't seen her . . .

He has.

Remembering this sent Karin's face an even deeper shade of red.

She'd been forced to wear a bikini during a temporary job earlier in the summer, without a shirt or skirt to hide things away. And the bikini top almost had . . .

"Karin? You've turned bright red."

"It's nothing!"

"So," Hidemi was nonplussed, "Sky Land?"

Karin panicked again. She had turned down the water park, but she hadn't decided about the amusement park.

"Um, I . . ."

"No? Is your boyfriend going to be mad if you go out with me?"

"My boyfriend?" Karin's voice went up an octave.

"The one with the eyes—tall with short brown hair?"

"You mean Kenta? He's not my boyfriend!" Karin looked around the restaurant, hoping none of the other staff had heard this. Kenta would hate it if everyone thought they were going out. "He's just a friend!"

"I think he's in love with you. He's been glaring at me all evening."

Karin's heart was beating so loud that she was sure they could hear it outside. Was he really jealous of Hidemi?

"Why are you smiling?"

"No reason!" she spluttered.

Karin risked a glance at Kenta, who was busy wiping down a table. His attention was focused on his work, although Karin had been chatting with Hidemi far longer than seemed acceptable.

Kenta wouldn't be jealous of me. I'm just a fool. After all, she thought, it had been Kenta who had given her the chance to talk to Hidemi by giving her the order.

"Like I said, he always looks like that," she said breezily. "I don't think he's glaring. He's just a friend. I'm sure he didn't mean anything by it."

"If you're sure. So, about tomorrow . . ."

Karin hesitated again.

Hidemi ran a hand through his unruly hair, a mixture of disappointment and awkwardness on his face.

"No?" he asked at last. "I suppose it's a little inappropriate, inviting you out when we've just met. I'm sorry."

"I didn't think that at all!" Karin said a little too hastily. Hidemi had saved her the day before and had been worried about Anju. Overall, he had made a great impression—if only her blood rush didn't surge when he was around. . . .

I really hope his unhappiness isn't my father's fault! That bothered her most of all.

Hidemi had saved her from the molester the day before. If the unhappiness he bore had been caused by her family, Karin couldn't simply ignore it. She had to make sure. Going to the amusement park might give her the opportunity to learn the truth, she reckoned.

"This isn't my only job, and I have summer school. I was trying to figure out my schedule. It should be fine, though," she said. "I think I'm free tomorrow."

Hidemi beamed. "Great!"

Karin smiled back and nodded. She was worried about her blood rush, but she was still pretty far from her limit. It wasn't as if she had anything against the teacher, and she hadn't been to an amusement park in a very long time. She gave Hidemi her cell phone number and left him to his meal.

Karin shot a glance at the clock and saw that her shift was ending. She had to get ready to leave quickly, or she'd be late for her next job. She didn't see the boss anywhere, so she called out to a coworker.

"Watanabe, it's time for me to leave."

"All right. You know that guy?"

"Sorry. We got to talking . . ."

"No problem. We aren't busy, and the boss isn't here. You enjoy all the dates you like."

"It wasn't a date! I barely know him!"

Karin stomped down the hall toward the locker room. Her face was red from Watanabe's teasing.

Bah! I talked with him for a minute. How is that a "date"? Or did she mean the amusement park tomorrow?

Karin froze. We're going to the amusement park tomorrow, the two of us. . . . That sounded a lot like a date.

No! Why did I say "yes"? Karin's face caught fire. Her mind had been so focused on her blood rush and Hidemi's unhappiness that it never occurred to her this might be a date. Karin hadn't ever been on a date. She hadn't even spoken to a boy in private until Kenta transferred to her class.

Oh, no! I can't turn him down now, though. What should I do?

She was closer to Kenta than any other boy, yet she'd never been out with him alone. And she'd met Hidemi only the day before! She didn't think he was a bad person. Still . . .

Calm down. Calm down. My heart's gonna burst!

The blood rush was bad enough; with this excitement on top of it, her heart was pounding.

Right! I'll talk to Anju! He works at her school. She'll know what he's really like!

The thought helped her calm down again.

Karin took out her phone and sent a quick text message to her little sister, asking her to be home that evening.

She'll be able to tell me if it's safe to go out with him tomorrow.

Karin didn't dwell on how pathetic it was that she was about to ask her fifth grade sister for dating advice. The only thing occupying her mind was the sheer terror of going somewhere with a man she barely knew.

Visions of Kenta suddenly swirled unbidden into view. *I'm sure he wouldn't think anything of it,* she thought. *I'm sure he doesn't think of me as anything but a friend. He wouldn't care if I went out with Mr. Kijima. . . .*

For some reason, she sighed.

I'm home! Anju? Ouch!"

Anju wearily closed her book at the thunderous arrival of her older sister. She let out a preemptive sigh and padded out to the foyer. As expected, Karin was lying on the floor, both hands clutching her foot. She had stubbed her toe while changing into her house slippers.

"Not here for a minute and already you're making noise. How long have you lived in this house? Learn where things are, you klutz."

The voice came not from Anju, but Boogie. The small doll clutched in her arms contained the ghost of a serial killer—a revelation that constantly terrorized Karin.

"And you reek of garlic!" the doll continued. "Keep back! The stench will get into Anju's clothes!"

Karin sniffed a lock of her hair in surprise. The faint odor of garlic lingered on her skin and hair; although it wouldn't bother a normal human, it could agitate a vampire's delicate sensibilities.

Anju stared at Karin in silence.

"I'll take a shower." Karin slid past Anju and hopped down the hall on her good foot.

Anju swiveled on her heel and went back to the living room.

"Karin went to take a bath," she said.

"Then, we'd better put this away," her mother responded. Carrera indicated a series of hefty leather bound books stamped with gold titles; however, she made no move to help.

"Henry," she said languidly. "Take those to the archive in the basement. Hurry now, before Karin comes back. And I'm a little thirsty. When you've done with those, swing by the kitchen and bring me a little chilled blood."

"Certainly. I shall be but a moment."

Carrera's husband towered over the rest of the clan. His dour looks and black goatee gave him an imposing presence, yet he obeyed his wife's every whim like an eager puppy. He left the living room cradling every book in his arms. Carrying a dozen heavy books was no more difficult for Henry than carrying a lunchbox, thanks to the preternatural strength with which all vampires were imbued.

Anju put her hand on the back of the armchair and looked into her mother's face.

"Mama, you and Papa were searching for something in those old books again, weren't you? Was it something to do with Karin?"

"Mm," Carrera responded absently. They obviously hadn't found anything of use.

"Karin is entirely human," Anju whispered, "aside from her blood rush. She loves sunlight and is afraid of the dark. Her sense of sight and smell are no stronger than a human's. And she can't erase the memories of those she bites!"

"Yes. You've been able to take care of her during the day so far. Once your powers fully awake, though, you'll be trapped inside like the rest of us." Carrera turned to face Anju. "Don't worry. That's why we allowed this human boy, Kenta Usui, to know the truth. We can't put this all on you."

"Still, at this rate, it seems certain Karin will be left on her own in the daylight world. . . ."

This thought was exactly why Carrera had taken the bold step of bringing Kenta into the family's circle of trust. So far, he had kept things secret and had been there to cover for Karin when she made mistakes in public. Not everything was going according to plan, however.

"Here you are, Mother: fresh liar's blood, chilled to perfection." Henry swept through the door with a silver tray balanced on one hand. Blood pooled in an elegant wine glass—the blood of liars, which Carrera adored.

"I took the liberty of chilling the glass," Henry continued. "Drinking hot blood directly from the veins of a human is a wonderful thing—but in summer, it's so much better chilled."

Carrera took the glass and held it to her lips. The contents scarcely touched her tongue before she spat it out. "Henry! The blood of a high school student who told his parents he was going to cram school and instead hung out with his friends at a convenience store is the penny candy of liars! How could you have imagined I would enjoy that?"

"I couldn't find anything better!" Henry protested. "I know, I'm sorry! Please, forgive me! Next time, I won't give up until I've found something properly dry."

Anju left the living room. Her parents were a loving couple, despite appearances, and they didn't need their children intervening. She carried Boogie down the hallway. The sound of slippers and the scent of soap followed her. It was Karin, changed into new clothes. Her damp hair gleamed in the half-light.

"Do I still smell like garlic?"

"You're fine," Anju sniffed. "I wouldn't go into the living room now, though. Mama is handling Papa. The blood he served her was nasty, so she's in a mood."

"What about Ren?"

"He didn't come home—staying with his new girl."

"Again?"

"What did you want to talk to me about, Karin?"

"Right. Anju, do you know Mr. Kijima?"

"Kijima?"

"Hidemi Kijima. He teaches at Aoba Elementary as a substitute—fourth grade, I think he said."

"Oh, right." Anju nodded. He taught a different grade, she missed a lot of days, and most students called him "Hide" for short, so she hadn't recognized his last name.

"How do you know him?" she demanded.

"I'll tell you all about it in my room."

Anju's room was stuffed full of dolls as terrifying as Boogie, and Karin avoided the place as much as possible. Anju had no such compunction about Karin's room, so the two sisters soon found themselves sitting on Karin's bed.

"So, what about him?" Anju asked finally.

"Yesterday, he saved me from a molester on the train. He recognized me from seeing me with you. He thought we were friends. Anyway, I told him we were sisters, and he said he thought you were isolated from the other girls in your class. He's worried you might be being bullied."

"Heh."

Karin wiped her brow. "He asked me to talk to you, to see if you had any problems."

"You? Help Anju?" Boogie snorted with derision.

"Not me! That's what Mister Kijima said!" Karin wailed. She was well aware that her relationship with Anju was topsy-turvy, but she resented the implication that she couldn't do anything for her sister.

"He doesn't need to worry about bullies," Anju said diplomatically. "I don't have friends among the girls and I don't care. So, what's the problem?"

Karin slumped with embarrassment. "I know he isn't your teacher, but do you know him well?"

Anju looked puzzled. The conversation didn't seem worthy of a special meeting to her.

"Did he say something to you? Is he angry because I miss so much school?"

"No, it's nothing like that. He was worried you were allergic to sunlight! He's nice. I can feel his unhappiness, though. My blood rush kicks in when I'm near him. I seem to be able to handle it unless he sees someone in long black clothes, and then it goes into overdrive."

"Black clothes?"

"He seems to have a traumatic memory involving a black coat or cape. He doesn't remember anything clearly. Do you think it's possible he was attacked by a vampire in the past and had his memories erased? Could he have retained the fear?"

"I think you're reading too much into it," Anju said.

"Papa always wears a black cloak when he's hunting!"

"A lot of people wear black coats in the winter," Anju pointed out.

"True. But Mr. Kijima also remembers the smell of blood!"

Anju frowned. "How do you know all this if you met him on the train yesterday?"

"Well." Karin took a breath. "Mr. Kijima came into Julian earlier today, by sheer coincidence. He saw a cosplayer in a black cape and got a headache, so . . ."

"It isn't like he figured out you're a vampire, then. Forget all about him. If you keep your distance, there's no problem with your blood rush."

"I can't do that!" Karin wailed, breaking out in a sweat. "I promised to go out with him tomorrow!"

Anju stared blankly, unable to comprehend how someone as man-shy as Karin had managed to swing a date.

Karin wiped her forehead and prepared to mount a defense. "He said he had free tickets for Shiinoki Sky Land, good until the end of the month. He invited me to thank me for showing concern about his headaches. I somehow ended up saying 'yes.'"

"Hm." This made sense to Anju. Between her sister's incapacity to speak coherently to men and the teacher's warm manner of speaking, there was no chance of a cogent refusal. Why would Mr. Kijima invite her, though? Someone with his personality must already have a lot of friends—and if his term was nearly up, it didn't make much sense for him to be inquiring about someone else's students. Either he saw Karin as nothing more than a harmless friend, or he harbored more intimate feelings.

Anju knew the second option would be far too much for Karin to cope with. "Mr. Kijima isn't a bad person, Karin. . . ."

Anju stopped short of mentioning Kenta when another thought grabbed her. What if Karin needed a new daytime ally?

Kenta was becoming a risk. Karin nearly had bitten him a few days earlier when another blood rush had sent her over the edge. She'd stopped herself at the last second, exploding with a gushing nosebleed. Kenta had taken care of her while she was unconscious—but the family had found this a less than satisfying situation. If she couldn't bite Kenta, he was of little use when Karin needed to inject blood. The epic nosebleeds took their toll on her body and were to be avoided whenever possible.

And that, Anju knew, meant Karin needed to find someone reliable she could inject when her blood rush came during the day. It had to be someone who, like Kenta, knew of Karin's vampirism. Karin and Kenta both lacked the ability to alter people's memories, which generally ruled out a third party unless Anju or Ren were around.

Anju wondered if Karin was falling in love with Kenta. If her psychological resistance was strong enough to suppress her instinctive desire to bite, then there was no point in trying to convince her that she should. The next time her blood rush peaked, Karin probably still would not bite him. At least things between them were unlikely to turn romantic anytime soon, thanks to Karin's personality.

It took a crisis to move a heart in love. Perhaps having Mr. Kijima in the picture would spur Kenta into action. Anju racked her brains trying to recall details about the teacher. He seemed cheery and likeable from the little she'd observed him at school. She vaguely remembered something about him getting a little too angry when one of the students pulled a prank; the specifics eluded her, but Anju reckoned she'd recall if it had been anything too serious. Mr. Kijima was fair game, she decided.

"Mr. Kijima likes crowds and commotion. If he says it's all in fun, then it probably is. I wouldn't read too deeply into it."

Karin blanched. "Going to the amusement park alone with him . . . it's like a date or something." Saying the word "date" was enough to embarrass Karin. She stared at the carpet.

Boogie opened his mouth to speak, but Anju quickly clamped it shut. "You're thinking too much," she said. "Mr. Kijima is the kind of guy who probably has hundreds of casual friends."

"You think so?"

"There's nothing to worry about. Go and have a good time. You're being too high strung. Or are you worried about what Kenta will think?"

"Kenta is just a friend!" Karin barked.

"Try not to shout in people's ears, Karin. If you don't like the idea, call Mr. Kijima and cancel. Tell him it's too much like a date."

"I can't say something that rude! He's a nice guy!"

Anju shrugged, which spurred Karin to make up her mind. "Right. I suppose he did ask me as a friend. I was worrying about nothing. Thanks, Anju!"

"Good. I'm going to my room." Anju plodded out of Karin's bedroom, one hand firmly over her puppet's mouth. She didn't let go until she was safely locked in her own room.

"That really hurt!" spat Boogie.

"I didn't need you fouling up things," Anju admonished. "You were going to make fun of her for going on a date."

"Of course I was! I mean, it's so obvious! Or did you seriously think he was inviting her as a friend?"

"No. I didn't want you making fun of her, though."

"Why?" croaked the doll.

Anju toyed with her hair and smiled faintly. "Hidemi Kijima did not actually use the word 'date.' If he did that on purpose, it was very effective. Karin thought she was going as a friend, and accepted without a second thought. When she realized it was a date, she started to back away."

"What are you up to?"

"I thought it might be a good idea to try some other people. If Karin won't bite that boy Kenta, then why did we bother letting him in on our secret? We need to shake him up, get him feeling he would do anything for her."

"By turning this guy into a rival? What if Karin changes her tune? This loser seems a lot more aggressive than that other guy."

"That would be fine with me. Think about it." Anju smiled and tapped Boogie on the forehead. "Karin is a bit clumsy, right?"

"*A bit*? She's a freak show!"

"If she made a real mistake during the day, when none of us could move, how much could Kenta really do for her? He's a high school freshman. What if Karin got mixed up with the police? He's a minor, and she'd need an adult to bail her out."

"I see where you're going. This guy isn't merely an adult, he's also a teacher—an authority figure."

"Exactly!" Anju beamed triumphantly. "He could well turn out to be a very useful partner. If Hidemi Kijima were in love with Karin, then he would take care of her. He was worried that I was being bullied, so we know he's a good man—and observant, too. So, we'll keep an eye on him for a while. Don't make fun of her about this, Boogie. I mean it."

"First Kenta and now this clown? Are you telling him your secret, too?"

"It's much too soon for that. We have to make sure he's serious about Karin."

Anju smiled faintly again. Her garnet eyes glittered softly.

She didn't yet know whether she was throwing a stone between Karin and Kenta or if she were completely changing the flow of events. Anju didn't care about either of the boys. Despite appearances, all that mattered were her sister's feelings—and her safety.

Kenta watched as the little hand swung past the six. "Nine thirty!" he called. "I'm off!" He wandered in to the Julian staff room and made himself a cup of barley tea. It might be night outside, but it was still summer, and he needed to stay hydrated. Beverages were free at the restaurant. If he drank water at home, he would have to pay for it.

He glanced at the work schedule. He was working a morning shift at Julian tomorrow and would spend the afternoon at the moving company. Kenta noticed that Karin wasn't scheduled to work the next day. Once again, he remembered what he'd seen that afternoon: a little guy, maybe a college student, who spoke casually with Karin, grinning when he talked to her. She had smiled back—and not the kind of professional smile employed by all the staff when speaking to customers. She had meant it.

Karin's friend Maki once told Kenta that Karin had no immunity against men, but . . .

She could talk to whomever she wanted. It was no concern of his. At least, that's what Kenta told himself.

It didn't bother him. It shouldn't bother him.

When he had seen them chatting at the register and called out, he had been doing his job—leading the customer to an open seat. There was no unconscious jealousy behind his actions—absolutely none. That's why he had let Karin take the order—and pretended not to notice how long they'd talked. Naturally, he had looked their way a few times; after all, they were in the same restaurant. How could he avoid it?

Then, she had looked like she was having fun. The memory of her smile made him sigh.

At that moment, the door opened. It was Kaneda, who had been washing dishes in the kitchen.

"Hey, Usui! Get me a glass?"

"Here."

"Thanks. Nice guys get promoted, you know." She flopped down on the sofa and flashed Kenta a meaningful grin. "You saw her talking to him, right? You okay with that?"

"Why wouldn't I be?"

Kenta didn't particularly like Kaneda. She seemed to spend most of her time looking for an excuse to slack off work, and she gossiped at the drop of a hat. She'd seen him coming home from the public baths with his mother once and had spent the next few days telling everyone he was living with an older lover. He tried to explain, but nobody believed him. After that experience, he had put Kaneda on his list of "people to avoid." Considering she'd started the conversation, though, there wasn't much he could do.

"Don't be like that!" she squealed. "That guy was totally flirting with Karin. He was short, but the tan made up for it."

Kenta stiffened at the mention of the tan. Kaneda obviously was talking about Hidemi.

She cackled, pleased with this reaction. "You're gonna do something, right? You can't let a playboy like that get close to Karin!"

"Why should I get involved?"

"Because you're going out with her! Everyone knows!"

"We are not going out! Karin and I are just friends." His mind stuck on the word "playboy," Kenta frowned. "Or do you know something I don't?"

"How did you guess? Listen, I hate to gossip, but I don't want to see anyone hurt Karin."

"What do you mean?"

Kaneda leaned forward conspiratorially. "You forced it out of me. Gossip is so crass, but if you really want to know . . . that guy used to work at my niece's school."

"He's a teacher?"

"Yep. My niece goes to Koukaen Elementary School. Have you heard of it? It's a private school for rich girls, basically. I went to the sports festival there last year, so I remember him. He was passionate and cheerful—the kids all loved him. Then, last fall, he was fired suddenly."

"Why?"

Kaneda lowered her voice and inched closer to Kenta. "An affair: They found out he was sleeping with the mother of one of his students."

"Really?"

"He may look like a child, but he works fast. Maybe it's that baby face; if he looked like a player, he'd put girls on their guard. My sister said there were all kinds of stories. It created quite a stir. He slept with more than one mother; and if they tried to break up with him, then he'd force the whole class to bully their kids."

Kenta couldn't believe what he was hearing. "That's sexual harassment!"

"*If* it's true. It could all be rumor. That said, there's no smoke without fire, if you know what I mean. You might want to warn Karin. Anyway, I gotta get back to work. See you later!"

"You're not on a break?"

"Nah, just thirsty—it's not like we're busy or anything." Kaneda lifted her heavy frame and wobbled out of the room. Kenta realized she'd left her dirty glass behind, but he was too dazed to make her wash it herself. It was all too much to take in.

Kenta was especially sensitive to sexual harassment. His mother had been forced to constantly change jobs because of a series of inappropriate bosses. Now, his best friend was in danger of falling victim to the same thing. If this Hidemi person was like the men who made his mother miserable, Kenta couldn't let it go. But how would Karin take a warning? If he described Hidemi as a ladies' man, then would that make the teacher more attractive to her? Would she assume Kenta was jealous?

Kenta clutched his head in thought. Jealous? It was a ridiculous thought. They were friends; Karin could go out with anyone she wanted. Kenta tried to convince himself that a warning was unwarranted—but what if Hidemi really were bad news? He resolved to watch the situation for a while.

Kenta sighed as he walked through the hot summer air. He'd made up his mind; yet, for some reason, his feelings didn't want to fall in line. He couldn't get the image of a smiling Karin out of his mind. How could she smile so innocently at a person like Hidemi? He himself had started seeing genuine smiles from her only recently. Before that, she had avoided him in an attempt to keep her vampirism a secret. The more suspicious he grew, the more he had come across as a creepy stalker. Now, they had the reverse relationship: Kenta tried to keep his distance, knowing that proximity set Karin's blood flowing.

Her blood rush meant Karin usually was crying, scared, or flustered whenever he saw her. Kenta found that thought depressing.

The other day, her blood rush had hit a peak, and she nearly had bitten him. She caught herself in time and wound up spewing blood everywhere, eventually passing out. Kenta had stopped her when she tried to flee the scene. Maybe running away was easier for her. How could he convince her the safest thing simply would be to bite him and relieve the pressure?

Kenta was so wrapped up in his thoughts that he almost jumped out of his skin when someone called his name.

"Kenta? Kenta! Where are you going?"

"Huh?" He looked around him and saw his mother gathering the laundry. He had be so lost in thought that he hadn't noticed he was right in front of their apartment.

"Sorry," he said sheepishly. "I was thinking about schoolwork."

He stalked up the short path to the apartment, still thinking about Karin Maaka. Behind him, the gate clanged shut.

Hidemi Kijima took his eyes off the sports coverage and picked up the ringing telephone beside him.

"Hello? Oh. Hi, Mika." His flat voice belied unhappiness at hearing his sister's voice.

"Were you expecting someone else?"

"Not really, just being dumb." He and Karin had exchanged cell phone numbers; still, he had half expected her to be calling his home line. He'd imagined her calling him to say how much she was looking forward to their date.

"You're not dumb. You're a moron!"

"Did you call all the way from Osaka to be mean to me?"

"No," Mika chuckled. "I was wondering if you'd found a job yet."

"I think so. I had an interview at a private school today. I think it went pretty well."

"Private school again? Are you sure that's a good idea? All you ever get are temp assignments, where they make you slit your own throat if any disputes arise—even if they're the parents' fault. They don't think anything of sacrificing a teacher to satisfy the rich parents."

Hidemi sighed. "I know. I'm not exactly in a position to be choosy, though."

"If you do get the job, try not to get so worked up when you visit the parents' homes. One of my friends said you seem to bring out the mother in people. You're the type of guy older women fall for, so watch out." Mika was only half teasing.

"Could you not put it that way? You're creeping me out. Besides, you know I like shy girls." Images of Karin Maaka raced through his mind. She had seemed genuinely concerned about his headaches. That round face and those big eyes staring down at him, blinking nervously . . .

Hidemi found himself thinking about the next day. Karin seemed to blush easily, so it would be best to go on a ride that made them forget any nerves: a roller coaster—or maybe the go-karts. He hoped she didn't get motion sickness.

Mika's sharp tongue interrupted his thoughts. "Don't you hide behind silence! I can tell you're smiling. What are you thinking about?"

"What? Nothing!" he insisted.

"A girl?"

"No! Nothing like that!"

"Lie to me and I'll beat you to a bloody pulp!" Mika shrieked gleefully. "Don't even dream of hiding anything from me. Tell me everything, or else I'll tell Kiyo you've been giving me lip."

"No fair!" Hidemi wailed. Mika generally was on his side; however, their elder sister was a harsh sibling. "Give me a break already. I moved out two years ago! I can date whomever I want."

"So you *are* dating. That was fast. Didn't you just get your heart broken in April?"

"Who's counting? And no, we're not dating yet. I met her yesterday, and we're going to an amusement park tomorrow."

"Tomorrow?" Mika smiled on the other end of the line. "Will you be home tomorrow evening? Kiyo's father-in-law knows a guy who's running a private school in your area. She's going to see him tomorrow and ask if he can help you find something. She says you shouldn't count on anything, but she's wants to call you tomorrow night and try to set up something."

"I should be home by the evening. Karin's still in high school, so we shouldn't be too late."

"High school?"

Hidemi realized his mistake as soon as the words slipped out—too late.

"You're hitting on kids now?" Mika crowed.

"I didn't hit on her! It was nothing like that. I saw her being molested on the train yesterday—"

"And you joined in? Scumbag!"

"No!" Hidemi wailed. "I saved her!"

"Again? You may be a shrimp, but you certainly get into your share of fights. You're lucky he didn't have a knife. Are you trying to get yourself killed? Sooner or later, you're going to get hurt."

"I can't ignore a girl in distress. And don't call me a shrimp."

"You're five feet tall."

"I am not! And anyway, she's shorter than me. She's a little shy (and not nearly as arrogant as you are)."

Hidemi has muttered the last phrase under his breath, so his sister wouldn't hear. It was the most important bit, as far as he was concerned. Both of his sisters were much older than him and had treated him like a toy his whole life, which is why he couldn't stand strong women. Karin's naivety was exactly what he wanted.

And the fact that Karin was shorter than him didn't hurt. Despite her height, she was filled out in all the right places. High school girls seemed to be developing earlier these days, he thought. Hidemi dismissed the thought as inappropriate.

"You're being silent again!" Mika shouted. "You said something snotty about me, didn't you?"

"I did not. I said that Karin was cute. She makes my heart skip a beat, sends shivers down my spine, gives me goose bumps—the usual."

"Goose bumps? That's so weird. You're supposed to get those when you're scared. If she finds out you give her goose bumps, she'll dump you."

"Forget I said it, then." Hidemi cocked his head to one side, trying to work out why he would have said that. It was true Karin had a strong impact on him, but . . .

"When that guy was molesting her, she just teared up and couldn't say anything. Very shy, easily embarrassed . . . relaxing to be around . . . You'd knock out a molester, right?"

"Only because I'm experienced," Mika said. "In high school, I'd have been too scared to do anything. I'm sure you remember me being that young."

"I was in kindergarten when you were in high school," Hidemi pointed out.

"That's right. Remember when you fell in that ditch? I think Nanae next door made you cry. And remember that time you and Hitoshi both fell in when you had that fight—and also when you fell off your tricycle?" Mika paused. "Come to think of it, you ended up in that ditch a lot."

"Don't laugh." Stories like that were why the age gap hurt. Hidemi was too young to recall any of the stupid things Mika had done as a child.

"Anyway, Kiyo is going to call you tomorrow. If you can't find a job, stop being stubborn and just come back to Osaka."

"After ignoring Dad and becoming a teacher, anyway? How can I?"

Mika sighed. "You are such an idiot, Hidemi. You always were his favorite. Dad may have given up on you becoming a doctor and taking over his practice, but he'd hire you in a second if you ever came back. You could learn a few tricks and become an accountant. You should do that." Her voice grew sweeter and sweeter, almost wheedling.

Hidemi let a long silence pass.

"We'd all feel more comfortable with one of us looking after the books," his sister said at last. "Of course, it puts all the blame on you, as well."

"I would end up being your slave!" he roared.

"That's what little brothers are for."

"Ha!" Hidemi smiled. "You almost had me going for a moment. I'm not going to stop teaching. I'll find something."

"You want to act like a big brother to all those kids because you're the youngest at home. You prefer elementary school because none of the kids are going to be taller than you, right?"

"Shut up."

"I'll tell Dad you've weakened," Mika taunted, "failed your job and lost the new girl."

"How do you know she'll dump me? Of course you attack when I'm weakened; my family is a pack of hyenas!"

Hidemi replaced the receiver and turned his attention to the television. The news had finished, and the screen showed a woman visiting a popular restaurant. He was too busy thinking about something his sister had said to pay much attention, though. Mika had seemed as if she were about to say something else, but what—could it have been about the molester?

He cast his thoughts back over the conversation, but it wasn't long before he once more was thinking about Karin. He knew Mika would have been furious to discover she was related to a student at his school. She probably would have asked why he hadn't learned his lesson at the previous school. That was a conversation he didn't want any part of.

Hidemi was leaving Aoba Elementary in another month. How could it be a problem? He had invited Karin to the amusement park on a whim, and she was so shy it would take a while before they got close, anyway.

A frown crossed his face as his thoughts skipped over to Kenta. Hidemi hated people like him. What did he eat to get so tall? And he was sure he hadn't imagined that glare. The longer Kenta stared, the more determined Hidemi had become to ask out Karin instead of simply eating and walking away. Besides, she was really cute. His heart beat faster just thinking about her. Hidemi wondered if attraction ever stopped feeling like a schoolboy crush.

He shook his head and looked back at the screen. A movie trailer showed what looked like a love scene, with a woman saying goodbye to a man on a riverbank before running away in tears. The man ran after her and threw his arms around her from behind. The character wore a long black coat, which flapped in the wind like a cape.

Hidemi clutched his forehead with one hand and punched the power button on the remote control. "Why does this always happen?"

The man who'd asked for directions at the station, the cosplayer at the restaurant—anyone wearing flowing black clothes made him feel terrible, especially men grabbing at women. It was as if his body unconsciously rejected the imagery, giving him a throbbing headache.

Scraps of memory sprang unbidden from his subconscious: a man in a black cape, a woman screaming, somebody shoving his shoulder, falling headfirst, the smell of blood—nothing else. All he could remember was that it had been awful and terrifying, nothing more.

He shook his head to cast out the memories and plodded toward the bedroom.

Ho!" Hidemi shouted. A sharp report immediately followed, and a bag of potato chips toppled from the middle shelf.

"Another hit!" Karin gasped. They were outside the shooting gallery, and Hidemi had hit five times in a row.

"It isn't that hard. You want to try?"

"No way. I couldn't do that!"

"Watching is no fun. Here, I'll hold the popcorn." Hidemi took his prize from the stall attendant and held the gun out for Karin.

It did look rather easy, she decided. She traded the paper bucket for the rifle, holding it in position and pulling the trigger.

She missed.

"So close!" Hidemi enthused. "Are you trying to get that cat-shaped coin purse?"

"Ha! I told you I wouldn't be good at this." Karin tried to return the gun, but Hidemi refused to accept it.

"Now, now. Try again. You can't give up after only one shot. I'm sure you can do it. Relax your shoulders. Lower your hands a little. Look straight ahead. Good!"

Karin fired. This time, she scored a hit, and the box holding the coin purse toppled over.

"A hit! I hit it!" Karin considered this her first major victory in the fifteen years and ten months since she'd been born. Overcome with excitement, she flailed her arms around. There was a dull clunk.

"Ow!"

"Sorry!" She'd forgotten that she was holding the gun. Hidemi clutched his forehead, tears in his eyes. Karin had struck him rather hard. She frowned in dismay, but he waved aside her concern.

"See? You hit it—not me, the coin purse. Ha! Ow. You're a little . . . demonstrative."

"I'm so sorry! Does it hurt?"

"Nah. I'm fine. See? No lump."

The young woman behind the stall held out the coin purse. "Are you okay? Or does love make it all better? Here's your girlfriend's prize."

Hidemi smiled brightly. "She's not my girlfriend. We're just here as friends, right?"

Karin nodded, relieved.

She found Shiinoki Sky Land more fun than she had imagined. Most of the visitors were enjoying the water park because of the summer sun, so the rides had short lines. The log flume had taken about ten minutes, and the roller coaster and swings had shorter waits yet. After three exhilarating rides in a row, they'd headed for the game stalls.

"I still have bullets left," Karin said. "Should I aim for that stuffed animal?"

"You're never going to get that one. It's too big. You need a few friends playing to all shoot it at once. But you probably can get the smaller one beneath it. You've dropped your hands again. Raise them up, like this."

Hidemi demonstrated. He placed his hands on the rifle, narrowly avoiding contact with Karin. The caution impressed her, especially after the incident on the train. She'd also been the victim of "accidental" contact when handing out gyoza at the festival. Hidemi was such a gentleman that she found herself relaxing.

"Perfect!" he said. "Fire!"

Karin pulled the trigger. A stuffed rabbit toppled over. It was her second hit in a row. She jumped up and down excitedly.

"I did it again!"

"See? I told you!" Hidemi smiled as if he'd shot the rabbit himself.

Karin added a bead kit to her booty before finally walking away from the stall, arms full of prizes. Between the screams from the rides and the excitement of the shooting gallery, her tone had grown steadily less reserved. "That was so much fun! Thank you!"

She still hadn't managed to find out anything about Hidemi's unhappiness, though.

I can't just come out and ask him, she reasoned, *or I'd sound like a lunatic—especially if I asked him if he's ever seen a vampire. He claims not to remember much of anything, anyway.*

It was harder to work into conversation than she'd expected.

Hidemi hadn't seemed to notice her ulterior motives. "See how easy it is? What next? I see a bungee jump over there."

"I couldn't bungee jump!"

"I'm sure it'd be fun if you tried it. It's safe. They have a rope and everything."

"If they didn't have the rope, it would be nothing but falling!"

"Okay, no falling. In that case . . ." Hidemi spread out a map of the park in front of them.

"Hang on, I'm going to throw this out." Karin indicated the popcorn bucket before darting over to a trash can. What she saw on her return was the last thing she was expecting.

"I'm so jealous!" screeched a quivering voice as a cold hand stroked Karin's hair.

Karin jumped out of her skin.

The hand belonged to the ghost of a blood-soaked woman.

Karin screamed like a five-alarm fire.

Hidemi sprinted to her side. He stopped about three steps away and blinked.

Karin swung her head from the ghost to Hidemi and back.

"Oh."

It was broad daylight at an amusement park. Karin realized the "ghost" was the barker for a haunted house attraction. She noticed a few other people in similarly ghoulish makeup trying to lure people to the exhibit.

"Come on in!" hissed the barker. "The chills inside will vanquish the summer heat."

Karin's initial fright had not yet passed, and she instinctively took a step backward. The move caused her to bump into someone else.

"Come into the darkness, little girl!"

The new figure was a "vampire" in a long black cape, his face covered in pasty makeup. Karin screamed again.

"Hey, let go of her! You're really scaring her!" Hidemi yelled, knocking the newcomer's hand from Karin's shoulder.

Her heart surged, driving a deep ache through her blood vessels. *Oh, no! My blood rush!*

Hidemi unleashed another wave of unhappiness, like the previous day. The feeling rapidly spread through his being, driving Karin to the edge.

"Come on, Karin." He pulled her away from the haunted house.

"Okay!" She readily agreed with the decision not to go inside, but her blood rush spiked dangerously when Hidemi touched her. She leapt sideways to avoid his hand; he didn't seem to notice.

"I'm sorry," he said. "I can't stand black capes."

"Are you okay? Another headache?"

"A little." Hidemi grinned sheepishly. "It's so weird. I can't even recall what happened to make me react like this!"

Black clothes seemed to create an almost physical reaction in Hidemi—and that meant a physical reaction inside Karin. If he didn't level off soon, she was in trouble. Her blood vessels were screaming already.

My blood pressure is rising fast. After the jumps in the last two days, there must be an awful lot flowing around in there . . .

Karin wondered if she had been foolish to come to the amusement park. She wasn't at her limit yet, but one more good burst and she'd almost certainly suffer an explosive nosebleed.

Karin looked around and saw a bench in the shade.

"Let's sit down over there," she suggested.

"Okay. I'm sorry for making you worry. I'll be all right in a few minutes."

They made their way over to the bench. An electric melody played out as Hidemi sat down. He pulled a tiny phone from his pocket. "Sorry," he said, turning away from her and flipping it open. "Hello? This is Hidemi Kijima, yes. Oh, Director! Thank you for yesterday."

His voice took on a deeper tone.

"I work at Aoba until the end of September, so there's no reason I couldn't start in October."

Karin guessed the call was about the job he had been trying to line up for after his current term expired. She moved away, not wanting to eavesdrop. She decided to try to find a vending machine and buy a soda.

Maybe I could ask Papa if he has anything to do with Mr. Kijima's unhappiness, Karin thought. *I couldn't talk to him yesterday, but . . .*

Her parents slept all day, so their waking cycles didn't have much overlap with Karin's. After her mother had finished disciplining Henry for collecting inferior blood, he'd left the house to collect more, and Karin hadn't seen him again before she went to bed. She cursed herself for thinking she could coax information out of Hidemi. His unhappiness was dangerous for her, and it was far too sunny to rely on Anju for help if anything happened.

Karin sighed.

Suddenly, Hidemi's voice grew loud. "What do you mean, you've changed your mind?"

He sounded completely shocked. Karin could see the blood drain from his face despite his tan. "Why can't you hire me? This is completely unexpected. My last job? The reason I had to leave Koukaen Girls Academy?"

Karin's heart picked up a few beats per minute.

Hidemi had told her he had a job lined up after he left Aoba Elementary; it seemed the tide had turned against him, though.

His voice rose as he got more worked up. "That was a misunderstanding! False accusations! I didn't do anything! I explained this yesterday! I thought you understood. . . ."

It seemed the person on the other end of the phone raised his voice, as well, because Karin could hear it clearly.

"I do understand; when we took the matter before the board, however, one member strongly objected. I know it was all a misunderstanding, but some of the staff don't want the slightest chance of a problem. A private school like ours simply can't afford to have anything tarnish our name. We can't hire you against the wishes of the board of directors!"

"I see." Hidemi realized there was no point in arguing. "Well, thank you for trying at least. If you hear about anything else, please let me know."

He hung up and sat immobile, clutching his phone. Karin had no idea what to say to him, so she stood a short distance from the bench and watched nervously. Hidemi looked physically wounded.

Is he okay? She was worried about him. Her heart was beating fast, her skin was crawling, her head was spinning, and the back of her nose was growing hotter. . . .

Oh, no!

Just as it had been about to settle, Karin's blood rush came roaring back to life. Her vision blurred as a painful nausea filled the pit of her stomach. Her instinctive desire to bite someone and relieve the intense pressure welled up like magma.

Propelled onward by her instincts, Karin took a step toward Hidemi.

It was the height of the afternoon on a bright and sunny day, though, meaning Anju was probably asleep and wouldn't see a message if Karin sent one. There was no one to erase his memories if Karin attacked Hidemi.

I can't bite him! It would be the end of everything!

She stepped back, forcing her mind to work. Her blood vessels would burst any moment. She put a hand to her nose, just in case.

The movement attracted Hidemi's attention. He dropped the phone in his pocket and smiled.

"Sorry, I was miles away. Is something wrong? Are you okay?"

His smile faded to concern. Karin stood still, holding her nose. Her shoulders shook with each breath. She couldn't answer. The slightest movement could push her over the limit.

"Karin?" Hidemi took a tentative step toward her.

All her blood vessels swelled.

This isn't happening!

Karin turned her back on Hidemi and fled. She headed away from the crowds, toward the back of a building. Her moves came unconsciously.

"Wait! What's going on? Karin!"

Perplexed, Hidemi gave chase.

Karin ran faster.

Don't follow me! My blood! Blood rising! Heart bursting! I'm gonna explode! Please, let me leave!

She was unable to formulate words, putting all her energy into getting away from Hidemi. Her brain swam with excess blood. Karin lost her balance as her sandals slipped on the grass.

"Ouch!"

She fell flat on her face. A moment later, she pulled herself up on her knees. Both kneecaps stung. The impact seemed to reverberate along her blood vessels, which throbbed with heat and excess blood.

"What's wrong? Are you okay?" Hidemi had caught up to her. His unhappiness stabbed at her like knives.

"No! Stay back!" Karin shrieked. She scrambled away from him, not bothering to stand. It was impossible to form intelligible words with one hand pressed against her nose, though. The single arm supporting her gave way and she nearly collapsed on the grass.

Hidemi was starting to panic himself.

"What's going on? You've turned bright red. And you're sweating! If you're sick, we should find a doctor."

The distance she had worked desperately to put between them vanished instantly.

Hidemi put his hands on her shoulder to help her off the ground.

Karin felt a burst of fire run from the point of contact to her heart, moving up her arteries toward her nose.

Oh, no! Here it goes! Her head spun and her consciousness began to ebb.

"No!" Something popped inside her nose, unleashing a torrent of blood that pushed her hand away from her nose.

"Yikes!" Hidemi leapt backward.

The propulsive force pushed Karin back to the ground, accompanied by the sound of a burst water main. Her field of vision turned red.

This is bad. He saw me . . . so embarrassing! A huge nosebleed . . . and no Anju anywhere!

Karin folded limply to the ground. The world turned dark, as if someone had drawn a black veil across her face.

"That's a lot of blood for a bloody nose," Hidemi said dubiously. "Keep your head up! You'll choke!"

Karin could hear his voice but struggled to make out individual words.

His final sentence shocked her back into cogency: "I'll call an ambulance!"

If she were taken to a hospital, they'd quickly discover she wasn't human.

"No, don't!" she cried, gesturing furiously at the mobile phone Hidemi had pulled from his pocket. "Please! It'll stop soon. No hospitals!"

"But—"

"This happens all the time." Karin fought to get the words out. "Please, don't call anyone. It's too embarrassing."

"Karin? Wait! Hold on!"

She had passed out.

Karin's head felt heavy.

My blood came spurting out in front of a stranger. Why isn't Anju here? I can't erase his memories on my own.

She felt cold and weak. Why could she hear marching band music? *Where am I?*

Memories flooded back as Karin sat up. She saw an unfamiliar white ceiling and tall glass windows. Rows of medical supplies lined the walls. It looked like the nurse's office at school, but she'd never been here before.

"Oh, you're awake."

Karin turned to find Hidemi sitting on a folding chair in the corner. He closed the book he had been reading. "This is the medical room at Sky Land. The blood stopped quickly, like you said. I brought you here because you seemed so adamant about not going to the hospital. I didn't call an ambulance. I told the staff you had a chronic disease and merely needed some rest."

"Oh." Karin took in his smile and sighed with relief. She had avoided detection yet again.

"You asked me not to call anyone, so I didn't contact your folks. I can do that now, if you'd like me to."

"No!" she blurted. Even if Karin were to call them, it would be too late now. They couldn't alter Hidemi's memories this long after the fact. She shook her head a little too violently, and the world misted over again.

Hidemi sprung from his chair. "You've lost a lot a blood. You need to rest. If you exert yourself too much, you'll fall over again."

"Yeah."

She didn't need to be told twice. Karin nodded and rested her head back on the cot. But the more she thought about it, the less relaxed she became. Hidemi had seen a fountain of a nosebleed. Her defect was her greatest source of shame. Kenta had begun to suspect her after witnessing a similar incident.

Karin found herself unable to think. The sudden developments had left her stuck in panic mode.

Hidemi broke the silence first. "So, that nosebleed . . . have you seen a doctor? I mean, you said this happens a lot, so it's obviously not the first time."

"It's nothing," Karin lied. "It happens about once a month, and it always stops quickly. Please, don't worry." She couldn't think of anything else to say.

Her blood rush *had* been limited to a regular monthly interval before Kenta transferred to her class. Now, the schedule was completely out of whack.

Hidemi coughed awkwardly. "How do I simply forget about a monthly nosebleed? I've never heard of anything like that. Look, don't get mad, but did this all start around the time you entered junior high?"

Karin shivered. How did he know that? Had he been studying vampires? She said nothing. Embarrassment and anxiety had her brain flashing hot and cold. Her face alternated between red and white at a dizzying pace. She pulled up the sheet over her nose.

Hidemi's voice grew more awkward: "Wow. I mean, you're already embarrassed, so this is going to be doubly hard to say—but I have to say *something*. Look, Karin, I'm just going to talk to myself, okay? Ignore me."

Karin had no idea what this meant; before she could make sense of it, he already was talking again.

"So, all girls get their period once a month, right? But then there's also something called *daisho gekkei,* which is really hard to explain. Basically, though, every now and then, there are people that find themselves bleeding from the mouth and nose instead of in the usual fashion. When they get their period, they also get a nosebleed. It's also called *hojuu gekkei.*"

Karin's eyes opened wide.

Humans have a disease that causes regular nosebleeds?

Female vampires didn't have periods. She knew enough about human biology to understand what Hidemi was talking about, though. She had learned about menstruation in health class back in elementary school. There had been a lecture for the girls. She'd also seen articles in women's magazines, and some of her friends had asked to borrow tampons when their periods arrived unexpectedly.

She hadn't heard either of these terms before, though.

Hidemi wasn't finished talking to himself. He sounded like he was wringing his brain, trying to squeeze out every last bit of knowledge on the subject.

"I don't know too much about it," he admitted. "I saw it in a book somewhere. And the force you displayed might suggest *hemangioma,* which is a sort of growth in the blood vessels. It's a benign tumor, but it bleeds a lot if it bursts. I've seen people taken to the emergency room after a hemangioma burst inside their nose. I know it must be embarrassing, but you should talk to your mother about it. And go see a doctor! Of course, I'm just talking to myself."

Karin relaxed.

Hidemi didn't suspect that she was a vampire. Now that she thought about it, she was a bit of an abnormality even among the creatures of the night.

Few humans would imagine the existence of a blood-injector.

Still, she couldn't figure out how Hidemi knew so much. Names and symptoms of diseases she'd never heard of seemed to flow so easily from his mouth—the same as when he had assumed Anju had an ultraviolet hypersensitivity.

Karin lowered the sheet a little. "You know so much. . . ."

"I didn't say too much and hurt your feelings, did I?"

"No, not at all!"

"Okay." Hidemi looked relieved. "I thought you might not want to talk about it, and I don't really know enough about it myself. My father is a surgeon. He runs a big hospital in Osaka. We always had medical books lying around the house. He had me reading them since I was in fifth or sixth grade."

"Weren't they hard to read?" Karin asked.

"A little. He started off with books on gynecology to encourage me. Don't look at me like that! Any boy would be interested! I'm long past those books now. They're much easier to understand." Hidemi paused, half embarrassed.

"My father wanted me to be a doctor," he continued. "I think he was trying to use the books to get me interested. I didn't want to be a doctor, but I liked to read—so, I read those books and a few others, as well. Now, I have all kinds of useless medical knowledge."

"Shouldn't you be taking over your father's hospital?"

"I'm the youngest child," he explained. "I have two sisters, about ten years older than me: one's a surgeon, the other's a physician. They can take over. Hey, your color's coming back. Can you move?"

Karin propped herself up on her elbows. "Yeah. I'm sorry. I always get anemic after a nosebleed. Were you here the whole time?"

"I bought a book to read. No big deal."

"What time is . . . Augh! I'm covered in blood!" Karin had looked down at herself for the first time. Her blouse was red with the dried product of her explosion, from collar to waist.

I can't go home like this! And what about Mr. Kijima?

She realized belatedly that Hidemi now wore a T-shirt with Shiinoki Sky Land mascot characters on it. He'd been wearing a dress shirt when they arrived at the park. Now that she looked closely, she could make out red spots on his faded blue jeans.

Karin tried to remember what she'd seen behind the red fountain: Hidemi, his hand on her shoulder, getting sprayed with a torrent of blood.

"Oh, no! I ruined your clothes, didn't I? I'm so sorry!"

"Forget about it. I'm pretty sure I messed up your sandals. Your toes don't hurt, do they?"

Karin blinked.

"I'm a bit too small," Hidemi said. "I'm not strong enough to carry you in my arms, and you were out of it, so I couldn't carry you safely on my back. And I didn't want to leave your bag. So, I sort of dragged you by the shoulders. Your feet might be fine, but your sandals dragged on the ground all the way here. Sorry."

He placed a paper bag on her bed.

"They weren't selling bottoms, but if you can change the top, it should help a lot. I'll just go buy something to drink and give you some privacy."

"What? Wait!" Karin yelped. She tore open the bag to find a Sky Land T-shirt. She called after Hidemi as he opened the door.

"How much was it? I can pay you back."

Hidemi stared at her before breaking into laughter. "Wow. That is so cute! It's only a T-shirt. Call it a trade for the sandals."

"Park shirts are so expensive, though!"

"Come on, now! Don't be so serious. When girls find out my father is a doctor, they usually ask for Louis Vuitton bags. I instantly break up with them, of course. My dad might be rich, but I'm not. Still, you need a shirt."

"Yes, and you already paid for the rides and food," Karin pointed out.

"Don't even compare a T-shirt with a designer handbag. It might be expensive for you, but not for me. Adults make a lot more money than high school students. I invited you out so we could have fun. I'm not going to get stingy about a T-shirt. That's too cute. You'd better watch out before I fall for you."

"Eh?" Karin gaped.

Hidemi made a face and covered his mouth with one hand. He avoided her gaze, flustered.

"Um, I hope you like the color. There were only two designs. I'll go get those drinks now."

He hurried out of the room.

Karin took the T-shirt out of the bag: It was plain black with the Sky Land mascot printed on the sleeve—different from the one Hidemi wore. He must have deliberately chosen a different design so they wouldn't match.

Karin tried to reconcile his gentlemanly behavior with his "cute" comment and blushed instantly.

He was kidding, she tried to convince herself. *I'd better change. How long was I out? I've been out for hours after a nosebleed before. Oh! The sun's setting!*

She could see the dusk gathering through the window and hurriedly looked at the clock. It was after seven. She had been out for more than five hours.

There was a knock at the door. When she answered, Hidemi and a Sky Land staff member came in.

"How do you feel? Are you dizzy? If not, we should go. The park closes in a few minutes." Hidemi turned to the staff member. "Thank you for everything."

The employee bowed and led them out of the room.

"I'm sorry it ended up like this," Karin said as they entered the warm evening air.

"Never mind that. You weren't feeling well and were simply trying to keep me from noticing."

"I was fine in the morning," Karin said. "The first half of the day was a blast. I don't know what happened."

"Well, that's a relief. Oh, not that way, Karin. My car's over here."

"I came by train . . ."

Hidemi cocked his head to one side and regarded her curiously. "That's because we were meeting here. I'll drive you home. In this heat and in your condition, I can't let you walk to the station, much less take the train."

"But—"

"You're too sick," he insisted. "What if you pass out again? It's not much of a car, but it has air conditioning, and you can lie down in the back. I have no problems being your chauffeur."

He obviously wasn't going to take "no" for an answer.

It wasn't manners that made Karin hesitate. She was afraid of a blood rush when she got near him, and worried that a human might find out where her family's vampire lair was.

After losing so much blood, though, her body felt heavy and her head was hazy. Her blood rush actually might help her recover. Karin resolved to have Hidemi let her off some way from her house so she could walk the rest of the way home; it was a technique she had used before. She accepted his offer and climbed into the compact car.

"Where do you live? Nishi-ku? Near the nature preserve?" Hidemi sensed Karin was too tired to chat. "Okay, I'll ask again when we're close. Why don't you go ahead and get some sleep."

Karin felt a wave of exhaustion crash over her as soon as she hit the seat. She instantly fell asleep, only to awake later to the sound of a ringing phone.

Not mine . . .

Her heavy eyelids wouldn't open.

"Hello?" Karin heard Hidemi from the front seat. "Hi, Kiyo. Sorry, we had a little trouble, so I'm not quite home yet. What? Turn up the volume on your end. I can't talk louder. She's asleep."

It sounded like he was trying not to wake Karin. The radio wasn't on, though, so even though Hidemi was whispering, Karin could hear every word.

"Oh, Mika already told you? Yeah, the girl I mentioned yesterday. Nah, we just went to the amusement park. She's nothing but at friend until at least September. . . ." Hidemi trailed off, as if realizing he shouldn't have said anything.

Karin could hear a flurry of indistinct questions coming from the other end of the line.

Hidemi sounded aggrieved when he answered: "Yeah, family of one of the kids at school. Her sister. Oh, let it drop. That's not why you called, is it? Come on, now! She's just a friend until I quit. Is that good enough for you? I haven't forgotten what happened at Koukaen. I'm the one who was framed."

That was the name of the school he'd worked at before. What had happened there?

"I can't help it! This stuff isn't logical. She's cute, I like her, and that's all that matters! Look, I'm driving. We'll talk later," he shouted, hanging up.

A moment later, he realized how loud he'd been. He anxiously looked in the rear view mirror, and he found Karin staring back at him, too surprised to pretend she was sleeping.

"You're awake?" Hidemi sputtered, trying to smile but failing. "You heard that, then? Of course you did. Um . . . Don't worry about it."

"Oh . . ."

Awkward. Karin had completely accepted the idea that they were just friends, but Hidemi had been ready to take the next step. He had been careful to keep things friendly, so she hadn't noticed. Or perhaps her lack of experience had made her overlook the signs.

Hidemi broke the silence. "That's the nature preserve. Where to now?"

"Go straight a bit more. Then, take a right at the light after the gas station."

"Okay."

It was completely dark outside now. The car rolled along empty streets, a few lamps here and there lighting the way.

"I'm really sorry you heard that phone call," Hidemi said apologetically. "I can't leave things like this, so I should tell you . . . I was fired from the school I worked at before Aoba."

He explained that the prior school had a serious problem with bullying, and he had gone to visit the homes of the students involved many times. One of the mothers had pursued an affair, but he'd turned her down. Mortified, she went to the school looking for revenge. She told the school officials that Hidemi threatened to make the other kids bully her child if she didn't do what he wanted. Gossip spread quickly among the other parents.

"I'll leave it up to you to decide whether you believe me. It isn't very believable, is it? I mean, you're the sister of a student, and here I am asking you out like this," he said bitterly.

"I believe you!" Karin answered hastily. "You're not the kind of person to sexually harass anyone."

"Thanks. You didn't come with me because I teach at your sister's school, did you? I mean, at first, it seemed like you didn't want to come at all. I thought maybe you changed your mind because of where I work. . . ."

"I did hesitate," Karin admitted, "because I'd just met you. I went with you willingly, though, and I had a good time. I was glad to make a new friend."

"'Friend' . . ." Hidemi sighed. "To tell you the truth, I didn't mean to ask you out that quickly. When that boy at the restaurant glared at me, though, I kind of felt some sort of stupid rivalry, and before I knew it . . ."

"Huh? It's not like that with Kenta!" Karin yelped. She waved her arms the way she always did when she was flustered, smacking them into the window frame. "Ouch!"

"They call this a 'compact' car for a reason," Hidemi teased.

"Yeah." Karin clutched her hand, tearing up.

"That clumsy thing is exactly my type," Hidemi said wistfully.

"It's stupid of me, I know."

"Nah, it's adorable."

Karin felt her heart skip a beat.

"Look, I'll be honest," Hidemi continued. "I've dated my share of girls. But when I look at you, I can feel my heart beating faster. I've never felt like this before. There's a strange tension, and the hairs on the back of my neck stand up. My skin crawls—no, strike that. Forget the crawling skin, that's weird."

"Forgotten . . ."

"Why do I keep saying stupid things?" Hidemi wondered aloud. "Where was I?"

Karin didn't know how to answer that question, so she hung her head and said nothing. Her own heart was beating faster than was comfortable. Karin didn't know whether it was her blood rush or the conversation.

"Oh, right: my beating heart." Hidemi grinned. "I know it's like some kid in love for the first time, and I know it's a dumb idea to get mixed up with a student's family, but is there any chance we could be more than friends?"

He sounded much more serious than he usually did. Karin could feel her cheeks glowing. She was sure she was red all the way to her ears.

A high school boy had asked her out once before. He hadn't exactly been in love with her, though, so it had been easier to deal with. What could she do now?

She didn't hate Hidemi. He was cheery and nice and fun to be around. If she'd had a brother like him . . . Her own brother was quite fond of Anju, but cold to Karin, writing her off as a defective vampire. Karin could talk to boys she wasn't related to as long as they weren't interested in her. She knew she didn't necessarily like Hidemi the way he wanted to be liked. She'd known him only three days.

There was a long silence, which was eventually broken by Hidemi: "This is all too sudden, isn't it?

Just friends, then. And if that's going too far, feel free to say so."

"Oh, I wouldn't . . ."

"Is this road ever going to get to your house? It's getting narrower and narrower."

Karin looked up. They were within striking distance of her house. Beyond this was a mazelike barrier established to protect the clan's lair. Humans who entered quickly would find themselves hopelessly lost. If she were with him . . . well, she didn't know what would happen. Karin hadn't ever brought a human home with her. She assumed the barrier would give way automatically. How angry would her mother be if she brought Hidemi home? Her nerves subsided instantly.

"Stop!"

Hidemi hit the brakes.

"Sorry! Cars can't go any farther. I'll walk the rest of the way."

"Wait," Hidemi said. "Let me get the door."

Karin picked up her purse and the bag with her bloody blouse. Hidemi dashed around the rear of the car and opened the door for her.

"I'll carry that for you," he offered.

"No! I'm fine! My house isn't far at all!"

Hidemi blinked at the ferocity of her response. "You're kidding me, right? I can't let a sick girl walk home alone at night—especially not in a deserted area like this. You passed out this afternoon, remember? I'll walk you to the front door and make sure nothing happens."

Karin's lip trembled. "But—"

"Don't worry about anything I was talking about in the car. Forget it. I'm simply worried about you. Please, let me make sure you get home okay."

"That's not it. My house is . . ."

Karin didn't know what to say. She couldn't tell Hidemi that her mother would yell at her if she brought a human into the vampires' lair, and she couldn't think of a legitimate excuse, either.

As she tried to think of something, a familiar voice called out: "Don't worry, Kijima-sensei. I'll take over from here."

"Anju?"

Anju was standing in the shadows by the side of the road.

Hidemi stared at her, astounded. "Anju? What brings you out here in the dark this late?"

"I'm training my pets."

Hidemi scoured the area for a dog but saw nothing. It never occurred to him that she was referring to her collection of intelligent bats.

"I'll take care of Karin," Anju said flatly. "You can go home now."

"Your sister's lost a lot of blood. She's not in good condition . . ."

The blank look on Anju's face never crumbled. She tightened her grip on Boogie and spoke with renewed emphasis. "Karin is used to anemia. There's color in her face, so she'll be fine. And our father is very strict. If he caught her coming home with a man, he'd be furious."

Hidemi took a step back. "That would be bad."

Karin bowed her head. "I'm sorry about this. I really did have fun. Thank you."

"Goodbye," Anju added. "You should leave before Papa comes out."

Hidemi's shoulders slumped as he flashed a worried smile.

"Okay, okay, no need to threaten me. I'll head off now. You two be careful. I'll see you later."

The two sisters watched him drive away. Anju shuffled off toward the house, leaving Karin to jog after her.

"You had a nosebleed?"

"Yeah," Karin admitted. "He didn't suspect anything, though—he was worried I had some kind of disease. His family is made up of doctors, so he knows a lot about diseases. It was something called daishou gekkei, where humans get nosebleeds every month. He never thought I was a vampire."

Karin chattered when she feared a verbal smackdown.

"Something else happened!" Boogie snarled.

"Nothing!" Karin wailed. "Of course not!"

Anju raised an eyebrow. "So something *did* happen."

"Not really." Karin could feel her face turning red. She tried to avoid her sister's gaze, but it was impossible.

"You're awfully flustered. Did he kiss you or something?"

"Anju! How can you say that?"

"Did you go all the way?"

"Augh! Anju! You're way to young to say things like that. He just told me he loves me!" Karin clamped her hands over her mouth. He might be a substitute, but Hidemi still worked at Anju's school. Should she really have blurted out the truth?

Karin spun wildly, trying to cover her mistake: "He didn't mean to say anything until after he'd finished at your school. He knows it's a bad idea to get involved with a student's family members. But he said his heart beats so quickly when I'm around that he couldn't help himself.

"Bragging now?" Boogie jeered.

"I am not!" Karin shrieked. "My point is that he knows he's a teacher. He said we should stay just friends until he's finished at Aoba."

"They can hear you inside," Anju said quietly.

Karin stopped waving her arms around and covered her mouth again.

"Don't worry," Anju said. "I won't tell the school about him. He went to an amusement park with you; he didn't do anything wrong."

Relief washed over Karin. "Right. Yeah."

"Why are you so relieved? What self-respecting high school girl is relieved by anything a child says? You're pathetic!" Boogie barked the insults with rapid-fire precision.

Anju shot the dummy a stern glance. "Ren isn't home, but Mama and Papa are in the living room."

Keen hearing was another vampire trait Karin lacked; somehow, her sister could tell who was home simply by standing in the foyer. Karin wandered into the living room to say "hi" to her parents.

"I'm home!"

"Welcome back, Karin."

"You weren't working today. Where did you go?"

Karin bounded onto a sofa. "An amusement park called Shiinoki Sky Land. It was so much fun! I'd never won a prize at a shooting gallery before!"

"With whom did you go?" Carrera asked.

"With whom?" Karin echoed. She hadn't anticipated having to answer that question.

Henry leapt up from an easy chair. "Was it that Usui boy? You're already dating? Did he make you do anything funny?"

Karin's mouth fell open. "No! Don't look at me like that, Papa! He wasn't there."

"That's a new shirt," noted Anju. "Did you buy it today? Where did you change?"

The questioning riled up Henry, who practically foamed at the mouth now. "You changed clothes? What happened? We never asked him to do that! Curse that Usui boy! How dare he! And with my daughter!"

Karin threw herself on her father to prevent him from flying off and strangling Kenta. "Where are you going? Stop!"

Henry was a full-blooded vampire, far stronger than his daughter. He dragged her across the living room floor with every stride.

"It wasn't Kenta Usui! I swear!"

What finally stopped Henry was the slipper Carrera aimed at his head. The force of the throw knocked him to the floor. Karin's mother then turned to face her eldest daughter.

"I can smell dried blood in that bag. You had a blood rush, didn't you?"

"Yes," Karin replied, feeling small. "It came out before I could bite anybody. I got blood all over my shirt, so I changed at the first-aid station."

"Why didn't you say so in the first place? I was so worried."

"You didn't listen to me, Papa!"

Carrera frowned. "Don't be too relieved, Henry. She must have spent half the day unconscious. Otherwise, why would she be up and about so soon? How did she explain things without any of her family around? I doubt your daughter had saved enough money to buy an overpriced T-shirt, so who paid for it?"

Karin gulped. Her mother's reaction wasn't as dramatic as her father's, but it was far more accurate. Karin looked around for help. Anju, of course, had vanished. *Typical!* she thought. *Stirring the pot and running away!*

Carrera's eyes flashed intently. "Tell me the truth, Karin!"

"Okay, I'll tell you! Stop looking at me like that!"

Karin told her parents the entire story, beginning with Hidemi and the molester on the train and wrapping up with meeting Anju outside the house. She made sure to mention how Hidemi had assumed she had some rare disease and glossed over the talk about future dates.

"I think I recovered so quickly because Hidemi was sitting next to me," she said. "When I'm with him, my blood rush gradually increases. I don't know why he's so unhappy. . . ."

"And this Hidemi Kijima is a teacher at Anju's school," Carrera said thoughtfully.

Henry paced back and forth, having sprung up from his chair during the story of the molestation episode.

"What is this world coming to? If I had been there, this Hidemi person never would have gotten involved in the first place. That molester would have died on the spot. I wouldn't allow a monster like that near my daughter! You poor thing; it must have been terrifying! I'll never forgive him. I won't allow this pervert to live another day! What did he look like? Tell me, Karin!"

Karin covered her face with her hands. The memories were much too embarrassing, and her cheeks were glowing. "Please, stop talking about it! I don't remember what he looked like! I never looked at his face."

"From what Karin tells us, this Mr. Kijima sounds like an upstanding individual. He saved her from a molester and took care of her after her nosebleed. He even bought her replacement clothes and seems to have been above board. It's more than most humans would do."

"He did too much, Carrera!" Henry countered. "He was after something. What a world! First, that Kenta boy—and now, another man has his shadow over Karin!"

Karin wrung her hands. "Gross! Stop talking like that, Papa! Kenta and Hidemi are just friends!"

She was glad she'd kept quiet about their conversation in the car. She knew if she had breathed a word of it, her father would be on Hidemi in a flash.

Carrera waved a hand, indicating she was through with the conversation. "Ignore your father, Karin. Mr. Kijima sounds like he's up to something, I agree, but you've known him only three days. Be careful he doesn't find out anything more."

"I know."

"Carrera! You're going to allow them to have relations?"

"'Relations'? What are you talking about, Henry? They scarcely know each other. We can decide what type of man he really is after we've observed him a bit more. In the mean time, that blouse isn't going to wash itself."

Karin gripped the bag and headed out of the room. "I'll take a bath, as well."

Carrera settled back in her armchair, speaking quietly to calm her pacing husband. "Henry, why have you not gone out to collect blood?"

"You aren't coming?"

"The moon is too white. I want a big red moon, to give it the proper atmosphere. Now, run along, and don't you dare come back with cheap liar's blood like yesterday!"

Henry left the room smiling.

Before heading out, he decided to have a chat with Anju, whom he found sitting on her bed, brushing her curls.

"Anju? What is your impression of this Hidemi Kijima from your school?

"He doesn't teach my grade, so I hardly know him. He seems cheerful and open, though. Everyone likes him." This is what she had told Karin the day before.

Now, she added one other thing: "If he bothers you, why not take a look in person? You can see him if you stop by the pool tomorrow. He's in charge."

"The pool is open in the evening?"

"No, but if you go right after sunset, he might be cleaning up still," Anju said.

"I'll do that. It all sounds above board, but a father needs to know for sure." Henry was fixated on thoughts of Karin, so he didn't see Anju grab Boogie's mouth and twist it shut.

"First, that Kenta kid, and now, another boyfriend. Even if she *is* a defective vampire, she is still the eldest daughter of the glorious Maaka family—the daughter of Henry and Carrera Maaka. It's natural that men are drawn to her charms, but it's a father's job to root out foul pests buzzing around her. Nothing keeps one hopping like a popular daughter!"

He left laughing, and Anju released Boogie.

"Ow! So mean, Anju!"

"You were going to ruin everything!" she hissed.

"How do you know? You're the one that put the two of them together. And now you're lighting a fire under your father? No father on Earth *ever* wanted his daughter dating *anyone*. Won't he get in the way?" Boogie spoke with his familiar cracked voice.

"I doubt it. And I want to be sure. I could have sent Mama or Ren, but I thought Papa would be faster. And as I expected, he plans to go see him."

"What is it you want to be sure of?"

"Hidemi's reaction. I might be reading too much into this, but maybe I'm not the only one who's confused."

Anju said nothing else, instead putting down her brush and staring into space. Her expression was the vexed concern of a student trying to solve a mathematical proof, only to realize she had missed an important condition.

 **CHIBI VAMPIRE
AND KENTA'S FURY**

Good morning! Karin Maaka, reporting for duty!"

Karin stood in the main hall of Julian and saluted. Having gone to bed early, she now felt as if she had recovered completely. She'd tried to get to work early—but by the time she arrived, the restaurant already was full with staff trying to get ready for the morning rush.

"Maaka! Can you help me wipe down over here?" Kobayashi called.

Karin wandered over and picked up a rag.

Kobayashi leaned over with a heavy smirk. "Did you have fun on your date?"

"What are you talking about?"

"Ha! Be that way. I saw you at Sky Land yesterday. He's in college, right? I saw you two getting into the same car in the parking lot."

Every pair of ears in Julian pricked up.

"What?"

"Karin had a date?"

"Who with?"

As the restaurant had no customers yet, all the girls gathered around Karin. Kobayashi chuckled and held court.

"Yeah, my kids and I were at Sky Land yesterday and we saw her and her date."

The girls grew more excitable.

"Who was it?"

"Kenta?"

Karin broke into a sweat. She had to put a stop to this.

"It wasn't him!" she wailed.

"Aw, I think you and Kenta would make a cute couple."

"He's just a friend!" Karin insisted. "We're in the same class and we live near each other, that's all."

"It wasn't Kenta," Kobayashi concurred.

Karin panicked. She had escaped the Kenta situation, but she was still in a tight spot.

"So, what was he like?"

Kobayashi took over. "He was kind of short, but he had big eyes and a cute face. He might've been about twenty?"

"Ah!" This sounded familiar to Watanabe. "The guy who came to lunch a few days ago?"

"I don't know. His hair was a mess and he had a deep tan—"

"That's him!" Watanabe crowed. "He came in the other day and talked to Karin for ages! So, he is your boyfriend!"

Karin interrupted desperately. "No! We did go out the other day, but it was as friends."

"If he's a *friend*, why were you wearing matching T-shirts at the park?"

Eek!

Kobayashi smiled triumphantly. "Like I said, I saw you. You both wore Sky Land T-shirts."

This seemed to intrigue the other girls.

"Friends wouldn't go for the pair look."

"Of course not. Come on, Karin. How far have you gone? Tell us the truth."

"We promise not to tell Kenta."

Karin's face was on fire. "Kenta has nothing to do with this!"

"Did you want something?" The manager bounded in from the kitchen, having overheard Karin's cry. He pointed at the register with a wide smile. "He's right over there. Did you finish fixing that shelf?"

"Yep. The screw had bent, so I replaced it." Kenta rose from behind the counter with a toolbox in his hands.

Karin and the other girls exchanged awkward glances. He must have heard the entire conversation.

"Time to open up!"

The girls scattered with a collective sigh of relief.

Karin resumed wiping down seats. *Why did Kobayashi and Watanabe have to say that stuff in front of everyone? They're so mean! I hope Kenta didn't get the wrong idea!*

She glanced down the hall, and her eyes met Kenta's. Before she could do anything, he turned his back on her, looking annoyed.

He definitely got the wrong idea. But it's nothing like that! Hidemi is a nice guy and a good person, but I don't think of him that way!

Karin ran out of the hall. She was sure Kenta was headed for the storage room to put away the tools. She ran down the back hallway—but just as she was about to put her hand on the back door, it opened from the outside. The steel door smacked her right in the face.

"Gah!"

"Karin? Sorry! I didn't think you'd be . . . Are you okay?"

Kenta leaned forward anxiously as Karin staggered, clutching her nose.

"I'm fine. It didn't hit that hard. Um . . . you know how they were talking just now? We weren't dressing to match! I got a nosebleed and soaked my blouse so Hidemi bought me a shirt."

Kenta tried to say something, but Karin was so desperate to clear up the misunderstanding that she didn't notice.

She kept right on talking without taking a breath: "There were only two styles of T-shirts on sale at Sky Land, and we ended up matching—but it didn't mean anything! He drove me home because I'd lost so much blood and wasn't feeling well. He's a very nice man, but it wasn't a date. Nothing like that! Really! He's still just a friend."

"'Still'?" Kenta asked.

Karin realized the implication of her words a moment too late. Hidemi's confession the night before—and his insistence she had time to think things over before committing—had been lingering at the back of her mind.

"I mean, um . . ."

She tried to take it back, but her brain was petrified by mortification. Nothing came out.

Kenta stood up and irritably ran his fingers through his spiky hair. He didn't move to help Karin up off the ground.

"Look," he finally said. "Whatever there is between the two of you is none of my business. You don't need to tell me about every date you have. I'm glad you know someone with enough money to buy you clothes. I wouldn't have been able to afford much more than a few tissues to mop up the blood."

Kenta didn't quite manage to hide the humiliation lurking behind his comment, but Karin was too flustered to pick up on it.

"Kenta!"

"We need to get back to work. We're almost open," he said, stalking off.

Karin pushed herself against the wall. Her legs were shaking, and she barely could keep her balance. *None of his business?* That phrase had stung. *Why?*

She herself had said something similar in the hall a few minutes earlier. But when Kenta voiced them, the words left a searing pain in her chest.

Kenta might be keeping my secret, but that's only because he believes all people have the right to be themselves, no matter whether they're human or vampire. It stands to reason he would say it's none of his business.

Karin chased the single tear running down her cheek with the edge of her apron.

The sun was starting to set, but the temperature remained steady.

The pool at Aoba Elementary was as busy as ever.

"Hey, boys! This pool is too small for that! Watch out for the little kids!" Hidemi wiped the sweat from his brow. Keeping track of the older boys was a chore, especially when they started racing down the length of the pool.

"Don't you want to swim?" A gaggle of fourth grade girls paddled directly beneath his lifeguard chair, tossing off the occasional question and generally making sure they were within sight lest the boys got too rambunctious.

"Come on in. Play with us!"

"You're gonna burn up there."

"Probably," Hidemi agreed. "This is hard work."

He took off his denim cap and covered his face with it. The two sports towels he'd brought with him both were drenched with sweat.

"I'd love to swim, but I can't," he added. "Once I started swimming, I'd have so much fun that I wouldn't be able to keep an eye on what the other kids are doing."

"Aw . . . "

"I completely agree," Hidemi said genially. "Look, you'll just have to have fun on my behalf. There are twenty more minutes until the pool closes."

The time warning was enough to spur the girls into action. They shot off across the pool.

Hidemi put his cap back on. The day was transforming into evening, and a fresh cloud cover was cooling the dusky air.

"Mr. Kijima."

The call came from the other side of the fence. Hidemi turned to find the speaker . . . and saw a severed head.

"Gah!" Hidemi shrieked, nearly falling into the water.

A moment later, a sheepish look settled over his features. The pool deck was raised a few feet, which meant that nothing more than a child's head would be visible over the fence.

Hidemi strode over to the fence.

His visitor was Anju Maaka. She wore a long-sleeved dress and cradled a frilly black parasol. The umbrella offset her platinum curls, adding to the illusion of a floating head.

"You startled me," Hidemi said as he reached the fence.

"You look pale."

"I was just spooked for a moment. Cooled me right off." He wiped cold sweat from his brow and willed the chill on his spine to subside.

Anju watched him with deep, thoughtful eyes. "You're scared of ghosts?" she asked. "Have you ever seen one?

"I'm not very good with ghosts. I mean, I haven't ever seen one personally, but I get chills whenever I visit a place famous for a suicide. Anyway, the pool's about to close."

"I'm not here to swim. It's my turn to water the gourds."

"Oh, right." Hidemi kept one eye on the pool as he talked to Anju. He knew he was shirking his responsibility, but it didn't look like anybody was in danger of drowning. He was about to give her gardening advice when Anju mentioned Karin.

"My sister wanted me to thank you."

Hidemi raised an eyebrow. "Is that why you came out here?"

Anju curled her lips into a tight smile. "Yes. She's much better today, so she went to work. She should be home by seven. I think she'll walk by the school, so make sure to say something if you see her. She's worried you're angry with her about yesterday."

"She shouldn't be. Anyway, I'll probably still be here at seven."

"Goodbye."

"Huh?"

Anju turned abruptly, as if losing interest in Hidemi now that her business had been completed. She headed toward the gourd patch.

"I don't get that kid," Hidemi whispered, wiping off another layer of sweat. He settled back into the lifeguard's chair and cast a sidelong glance at the fence.

A middle-aged man in a dark suit was talking to Anju through an open window at the school, someone Hidemi hadn't ever seen before. Anju appeared to be annoyed by the conversation.

An electric shock ran down Hidemi's spine. Something was off.

"I'll be right back. Try not to drown," Hidemi called out to the swimming kids. He vaulted the low fence and darted over to Anju.

"What are you doing here? This building's off limits to the general public," he snapped, addressing the stranger.

"Who are you?" the man retorted. He was in his sixties, encased in a blue double-breasted suit and what looked like an unusually stiff wig.

Anju used the exchange as an excuse to step aside.

"I'm Hidemi Kijima. I teach here. Are you someone's father?"

The older man peered condescendingly through the window. "A teacher? You must be new. I'm Nunoura, head of the educational council."

Hidemi gulped. He'd completely forgotten that inspections were slated for that day. He couldn't see the school gates from the lifeguard chair and had missed the inspectors' arrival.

"I'm sorry," he said. "What were you two talking about?"

"You said it yourself. This building is closed to visitors. I was asking the girl what she was doing here."

Hidemi grimaced. The visitor must have seen her blonde hair and violet eyes and assumed she'd wandered over from the international school. He waved dismissively at Anju. "It's all good. You can go."

The assumption of authority enraged Nunoura, who fumed silently. Anju ignored his obvious vexation and left quickly.

Hidemi turned back to his superior. "Don't worry, she's a student here."

"And you allow the children to come and go as they please?"

"They come to the pool in the afternoons. Some of the kids come back to water the plants and feed the chickens and rabbits," Hidemi said, pointing to each in turn.

"Enough!" Nunoura cut him off with a glower before stomping away.

Hidemi recalled that Nunoura was reeling from a recent divorce and decided he was lucky to get away with such a brief conversation. No sooner had the thought crossed his mind than he heard students calling from the pool.

"Goodbye!"

"See you later!"

Two of the older girls had climbed out of the water and were now waving goodbye.

"Take care!" Hidemi called out as he crossed back over to the pool. "Don't go off with strange men!"

"We know!"

"We're not babies!"

The girls walked past Hidemi as he climbed the stairs to the pool deck. One of them was nearly as tall as him. Hidemi had a complex about his height, so he hung his head dejectedly. He liked that Karin was shorter than he was.

Karin! Anju had said she might walk past the school on her way home. Hidemi doubted he would be lucky enough to see her. There were likely to be endless staff meetings following the inspection.

He considered calling her when a scream rang out from the gym: "Eek! Someone's peeping!"

Kenta heard the scream from the men's bathroom near the auditorium.

He'd worked at Julian in the morning, transferring to Black Dog Damien Delivery Company at noon. A plate of leftover cutlet sandwiches greeted him at his second job; shortly after eating them, however, Kenta realized they'd been on the table all night. His insides began churning a few hours later, and a delivery near the school had pushed him over the limit: He'd run straight from the truck to a school bathroom, clutching his belly the whole way.

He'd finally gathered the strength to rise up from the toilet seat when he heard the scream. The voice sounded quite near the bathroom.

Kenta hurriedly buckled his belt at the sound of approaching footsteps. The bathroom door opened before he could exit his stall. He froze at the sound of someone entering. But the door of the stall next to him remained silent, and Kenta didn't hear the sound of washing hands, either. Before he could figure out what to do, the door swung open again, and the echo of footsteps faded down the hall.

Kenta managed to catch a glimpse of the man's back before the door swung shut. He couldn't fathom the visitor's actions, but puzzling it out made him forget all about the scream.

While he'd been groaning in the stall, his partner had been carrying on with the remaining deliveries all by himself. Kenta quickly washed his hands and left.

A moment later, he realized he was lost. He thought he'd entered the school near the auditorium, but the grounds looked unfamiliar. Kenta wandered for a few minutes, finally throwing his hands up in frustration outside the gym. He was sure he hadn't passed it before.

"Hey! You there!" The angry voice came along with the patter of shoes on tile.

Kenta turned in surprise. He recognized the newcomer as the guy Karin had been chatting with in Julian a few days earlier.

"What—"

Hidemi grabbed him by the shirt before Kenta could finish.

"Was it you? Who are you? What are you doing here?"

Kenta easily tore free from the smaller man's grip. "What are you talking about? What's going on? Who are *you?*"

Kenta tore off his visor, revealing his face for the first time.

"You're the boy from the restaurant," Hidemi muttered. "I'm Hidemi Kijima, a teacher here. Someone peeped into the girls' changing room a few minutes ago."

"That must have been the scream," Kenta reasoned.

Hidemi suspiciously eyed Kenta's uniform. "You work for Black Dog Damien? What are you doing wandering around here?"

"I was using the bathroom, but I can't remember where my partner was going to pick me up."

"That's a terrible excuse. How can you get lost at an elementary school? It isn't that big."

"I guess I didn't pay much attention to where I was going. I ate some bad food and was focused on finding a toilet."

Hidemi crossed his arms. "I'm not buying it. Come with me. We'll see if the kids can identify you."

"Let go of me! I still have deliveries to make!"

As the two men struggled, a young woman in a suit hurried over. A trembling middle-aged man stomped onto the scene a moment later, wiping sweat from his brow.

"Mr. Kijima! What's all this?"

"Tsujikawa! I found this delivery guy loitering here and thought it could be our man."

The woman pushed her black-framed glasses to the top of her nose and examined Kenta. "The peeping Tom? I sincerely doubt it. The girl who saw him looking in the windows didn't see his face, but she said he definitely had black hair."

Kenta gave a sigh of relief. His own hair was brown.

"Oh." Hidemi let go of Kenta with a guilty sigh.

"Perhaps you should listen to the description before running off half-cocked," Tsujikawa continued.

"Yeah, but I didn't think he'd have had time to get very far. . . ."

"This impulsive tendency of yours to act without thinking through anything causes endless trouble. There are far better things you could be doing—contacting the children's guardians, for example; walking them home if their parents can't pick them up; coming to the staff meeting . . ."

The more the woman berated Hidemi, the more Kenta felt his anger ebb and sympathy take its place. The older man appeared to agree.

"Now, now, Tsujikawa. Mr. Kijima meant well. Instead of lecturing him, we should take care of those other matters. You too, Mr. Kijima."

The latecomers headed back into the building. Hidemi clucked his tongue in irritation.

"Now, Mr. Kijima!" the head teacher insisted.

Hidemi took a few steps after them, and then he turned back to Kenta. "Sorry. I really hate guys who prey on kids. I tend to lose my head around them. You really shouldn't be walking around a place like this unsupervised, though. Anyway, I think I see your delivery van over there."

Then, he disappeared inside.

The apology did nothing to wash the bad taste out of Kenta's mouth. His anger had returned. He stomped off toward the van and saw his partner waiting for him.

"Hey, Usui! Feeling better?"

"Sorry, Sakata. I got lost on my way back. Everything's in good shape."

"The summer runs are dangerous, man. You're almost off work for the day, right? Get some water, go home, and take it easy."

Kenta could only dream of going home. He was scheduled for another shift at the restaurant, and he needed the money. He wondered if Karin was still there, and then he remembered how happy she had looked chatting with Hidemi earlier.

The anger at being accused of being a peeping Tom came rushing back. Karin had said Hidemi was a good guy, but he didn't seem like that to Kenta at all. His excuse about hating predators seemed phony, as well. Kenta thought about his mother, who kept meeting nice men at work who wound up turning into jerks. And now, Karin seemed caught in the same trap. Why hadn't he listened to Kaneda?

Sakata dropped Kenta off behind the restaurant. He walked into Julian and was about to enter the men's locker room when the adjacent door swung open. Karin emerged from the women's locker room, wearing a summer sweater and a miniskirt.

"Kenta!"

"Karin!"

Karin awkwardly hung her head, remembering Kenta's hostile attitude earlier that morning.

Kenta felt equally awkward. His anger toward Hidemi soon overpowered his sheepishness, though: "Karin, that guy Hidemi . . ."

"What about him?" Karin asked nervously, peering up at him through her hair. She could tell he was furious about something.

"You said he was a good guy, but do you know what they say about him?"

"Huh?"

"I heard this from Kaneda; supposedly, he got fired from his last job for having an affair with a student's mother—and more than one, too. He forced them into it by saying he'd make the other students bully their kids if they refused. He's a sexually harassing scumbag, not a teacher."

"That's not true!" Karin fumed. "Hidemi told me the real story: He was framed. One of the mothers asked him out and he said 'no.' She got mad and started the rumors."

Karin trusted Hidemi Kijima. White fire went through Kenta's head at the thought, like a short circuit in his synapses. He couldn't stop himself from snarling a response. "You believe that? You have only his word for it. Of course he'd say that!"

"He saved me from a molester on the train. He doesn't seem like a perv. I got a nosebleed at the park, and he took care of me without trying any funny business. He's a cheerful guy. He's nice."

The more Karin defended Hidemi, the more Kenta became enraged. He knew full well nobody ever would call *him* cheerful. He couldn't afford to buy Karin clothing, nor drive her home.

"'Nice'? I'm sure he's nice to any woman at first, same as all the guys who harassed my mother." Kenta was too furious to realize his reaction was fueled by his own feelings of inadequacy and his mother's experiences.

"Kenta . . ."

"He's not so nice to men. About an hour ago, he accused me of peeking into the girls' changing room at his school, when I was merely lost."

Karin's eyes widened.

Kenta plowed on, without waiting for a reaction. "I told him I got lost on the way back from the bathroom while trying to find my delivery truck, but he wouldn't listen to me. He simply assumed I'd done it. I wouldn't be surprised if *he* was the one peeping and tried using me to cover for it. Maybe he doesn't stop at sexual harassment, maybe he—"

"Stop it!" Karin shrieked, cutting him off. "I can see you're angry at being mistaken for a peeping Tom, but that's . . . How can you say those things?"

Kenta swallowed his words. He could see tears in Karin's eyes.

"You know better than to trust anything Kaneda says," she continued. "Remember that time she was spreading stories about you? I can't believe you'd trust her word over mine. What's the matter with you? This isn't like you at all!"

The fire in Kenta's brain vanished as quickly as it had come. He hadn't realized how out of character he was behaving until Karin pointed it out.

The main reason his mother was forced to quit her jobs had been her boss' sexual harassment—but it wasn't the only reason. The other female employees often would gossip that she had slept with the boss to get ahead, half in spite. She never told Kenta the details, but he would pick them up from careless neighbors soon enough. His first reaction always was to want to start punching people.

And yet, here he was, acting exactly like the gossips that terrorized his mother.

He had been mad at Hidemi, but that was no excuse. Kenta fled to the men's locker room in embarrassment, unable to face Karin.

"Kenta? Kenta!" she called after him, but he didn't answer. He couldn't believe what he had done. The more Karin had defended her new friend, the angrier he'd become. Words he normally would have swallowed had come tumbling out. It was as if his brain had switched to autopilot.

Karin gave up calling his name. He heard her sandals pad down the hall, dragging limply.

There had been tears in her eyes when she was yelling at him. Had it really hurt her that much to heard bad things about Hidemi Kijima?

Kenta felt a deep sense of loss.

He sat with his back against the door, not even turning on the lights, and hung his head.

The evening star shone in the purple night sky. Karin walked alone through the deepening shadows, downcast.

Why? Kenta isn't the type to say nasty things about people. And Hidemi isn't like that at all. Why didn't Kenta believe me? Does he trust Kaneda more than me? The thought made her sad.

Maybe he doesn't care about me at all. That's why he doesn't trust me. . . .

She remembered what he'd said that morning: "Whatever there is between the two of you is none of my business." It was a cold way of putting it, but a friend naturally would feel that way.

Karin and Maki had been friends since first grade, but she wouldn't dream of sticking her nose in if Maki got a boyfriend. Unless the boyfriend were really a terrible, horrible person, she would respect Maki's feelings and say nothing. It made perfect sense for Kenta to say it was none of his business.

I would say that, too, Karin thought. *Kenta is just a friend, nothing more. After all, I'm a vampire—a whole different species. And my blood rises every time I'm around him. Everyone acts like I'm in love with him, but that's just impossible.*

She wasn't allowed to be. Ren had been furious when she'd suggested making Kenta happy enough that she could be around him without triggering her blood rush: "We are vampires! Human lives don't concern us! The woman you bit the other day went right back to her life of misery the second your blood injection wore off, didn't she? Don't be absurd!"

In a sense, he was right. Karin *was* a vampire, albeit a defective one. She had no right to think about trying to make Kenta happy. She'd done nothing but cause problems for him. It was amazing he still was willing to be her friend. That was more than enough.

Or so she tried to make herself think.

"Whatever there is between the two of you is none of my business." Every time she remembered Kenta's words, she felt miserable. She sighed, deep and long.

"Hey, Karin!"

Karin looked up at the sound of her name, surprised. Her mind had been somewhere else, and her feet had traversed the path toward home of their own accord. She realized she was standing in front of Aoba Elementary.

Hidemi had called out to her from the gate; now, he ran over. "How are you feeling?" he asked breathlessly. "You don't look well."

"I'm fine. I'm sorry about yesterday."

"Forget about it," Hidemi said, glancing up and down the street. "Have you seen any strange men around?"

"Strange men?"

"Someone peeped into the girls' changing room about an hour ago."

Karin stiffened. "Kenta said you thought he was peeping. . . ."

Hidemi looked guilty. "You heard? Kenta is the tall guy from the restaurant, right? I guess he told you. Anyway, someone opened the window enough to get a good look at the kids changing to go home after the pool closed. The girls noticed and screamed, so he ran. I was just getting back from supervising at the pool and was too late to catch him. I was so mad that, when I saw your friend wandering around the grounds, I jumped to the conclusion that he was the same guy. I'll have to apologize if I see him again."

Karin couldn't think of anything to say. After she had argued about the situation with Kenta, she was too drained for a second round.

Hidemi scoured the trees and bushes that lined the street, as if the peeping Tom were lurking nearby. "One of the teachers saw him looking into a second floor window an hour ago."

"The second floor?"

"Three people saw him, so it must be true. Maybe he was standing on a ledge or something. I hear the really dedicated guys can use shutters to climb all the way to the fifth floor. Keep an eye out if you're walking home. He could be in the area still."

Karin was struck by the sensation of being watched; when she turned to look, though, the street was empty.

"What did he look like?"

"I didn't see him," Hidemi admitted. "Supposedly, he's got a mustache and bushy eyebrows. If I weren't working, I'd walk you home myself. Are you sure you're okay? You really don't look well."

He gave Karin an encouraging slap on the shoulder. It was an innocent gesture that reminded her of childhood. The clenched feeling that had ached inside her since the fight with Kenta eased a little. A tear rolled down her face.

"Karin?"

"It's nothing!" she blurted, quickly wiping her face.

The voice that roared behind them shocked them both: "You made my daughter cry?"

Karin spun around to see her father gliding down from the roof of the school. The dim lights of the stars shone faintly in the sky, the sun having set a few minutes earlier. Henry's flowing cape made him look like an enormous bat.

"What?"

"Don't look!"

Karin slammed her shoulder bag into Hidemi's face. "Guh!"

The blow caught him off guard. Hidemi lost his balance and crumpled to the ground, his head hitting the pavement with a hollow crack.

"Eek! Mr. Kijima! Are you okay?" Karin gasped, crouching beside him.

Henry landed beside her. "Is he okay? You're the one that hit him, Karin!"

"Because you showed up out of nowhere!" Karin wailed. The shocking entrance had banished her tears. "Put that cape away! Do you want everyone to know you're a vampire?"

Hidemi wouldn't wake up no matter how hard Karin shook him.

"I didn't want him to see you flying, but I didn't mean for *this* to happen!"

"Once he's seen me, there's not much point in hitting him," Henry pointed out.

"Don't act like this isn't your problem, too!" Karin glared at her father. He bent down beside his daughter and took Hidemi's wrist, feeling for a pulse.

"Everything seems normal. It's probably no more than a minor concussion. The shock of erasing his memory should be enough to wake him up. We can't have him remembering what he saw. The last few minutes should be fine. . . ."

Henry moved to put a hand on the teacher's face.

Hidemi suddenly bolted upright, screaming. Karin clutched her father's arm in terror. They had no time to hide.

Hidemi looked around him, puzzled.

"Karin? What are you . . . Why am I here?"

He seemed surprised to find himself sitting on the ground, and he frowned at Karin and Henry.

Henry managed an awkward response. "Why are you lying on the side of the road?"

"Um. I . . ." Hidemi rubbed the back of his head, grimacing in pain. "I was out here looking for a peeping Tom, a big guy with a beard . . ."

He looked at Henry again. The description was a perfect match.

Henry didn't appear at all concerned.

"Allow me to introduce myself. I am Henry Maaka, Karin's father. You must be Hidemi Kijima. My daughters have told me about you."

"Karin and Anju?"

"Yes. Karin tells me she encountered a molester on the train the other day. I can't bear the thought of anything happening to her, so I came to walk her home from work today."

Karin nodded hurriedly. He was lying, but she had to support her family. There was an alibi hidden in his words, proving he wasn't the prowler.

"We saw someone lying by the side of the road," Henry continued. "Karin told me you were a teacher here. What happened? Sunstroke?"

"I don't know," Hidemi admitted. "Someone snuck onto the school grounds, so I've been out looking for him. Have you seen anyone suspicious?"

Hidemi stood up, brushing the dirt off his clothes. Then, he shivered, as if suddenly cold.

Karin gulped as the first twinges of her blood lust roared to life.

Henry had hidden his cape, but he still wore a long black coat. The ensemble was more than enough to draw out Hidemi's strange fear.

"We haven't seen anyone," Henry said. "Are you okay? You don't look well."

"No," Hidemi said, clutching his temples. "I was supervising the pool today and had sunlight glaring in my eyes all afternoon. Now that the temperature's dropping, I'm starting to feel a little woozy. I'm sorry. It's been a little dangerous around here recently. Please, be careful on your way home." He said the last bit more politely than usual. Then, he bowed and turned to head back toward the school.

Henry and Karin bowed in response.

Hidemi stopped suddenly. "Excuse me, Mr. Maaka? This is a weird question, but have we ever met before—a long time ago, maybe fifteen or sixteen years ago?"

Hidemi had turned back around to face Henry, but his eyes weren't focusing on the man. Instead, they seemed to be calling up a hazy memory. Every so often, they would focus on Henry momentarily, and each time, his face stiffened reflexively.

Karin waited for her father's answer. She herself had been trying to figure out how to ask the same question for some time.

Henry mulled it over and finally shook his head. "Not that I recall."

"Okay. Sorry."

Hidemi lowered his head just as Tsujikawa came running from the school.

"Mr. Kijima! How long—" she said, freezing when she saw Henry. A moment later, she screamed, "That's him!"

All three shivered at the sheer volume of her voice.

Tsujikawa screamed again. "Help! Everyone, I found the peeping Tom!"

"It's not him, Tsujikawa!" Hidemi rushed to her side in a frantic effort to defuse the situation. He reached out for her but timed the gesture badly. His hands grasped where they shouldn't have—which had the effect of pouring gasoline on a fire.

"Get your hands off me!" Tsujikawa shrieked, slapping the teacher as hard as she could.

"Ow!"

Henry and Karin stared in astonishment, unable to react.

A throng of teachers soon joined the quartet.

"What's going on?"

"He's the peeping Tom! Don't move!"

Henry raised a powerful fist. "You're accusing *me* of being a peeping Tom?"

"Papa! Stop!" Karin threw herself at his arm. Violence was the last thing the situation required.

Hidemi had recovered sufficiently enough from his slap to push himself between Henry and the teachers. "Listen to me! He didn't do it! He fits the description, but he's not the guy. This is Anju Maaka's father."

At this, the other teachers exchanged glances.

Hidemi pressed on. "He was walking his older daughter home from work and just happened by. He had no time to sneak onto school property. Right?" He turned to Karin for confirmation.

She nodded vigorously. "Papa wouldn't do anything so horrible!"

The protest seemed to convince the other teachers. Tsujikawa pushed her spectacles to the top of her nose and grudgingly apologized.

"Back inside, everyone," the principal ordered. "Members of the education council, I do beg your pardon. We should get back to the meeting."

But one of the visiting dignitaries harrumphed: "All this commotion over a case of mistaken identity. This school is slack all over, not just security. That girl earlier, with the flashy clothes and parasol . . ."

Karin and Henry looked at each other.

The man's scorn was not directed at them, but alluding to Anju had rankled. They lingered a moment to size up the newcomer. It was a man in his sixties, wearing a dark suit.

"Strange clothing is always the first sign of delinquency. Allowing a child to dress like an adult without precautions is parental neglect . . ."

"I beg your pardon, Chairman Nunoura," Hidemi said, stepping in before Henry could say anything. "That student wears long sleeves and carries a parasol because she has an ultraviolet sensitivity. That kind of allergy can be fatal. Her clothes are a medical necessity. It's unfair to brand her as a problem child based on her appearance."

"Oh? You know who I mean?"

"The child you were talking to earlier? That's Anju Maaka, fifth grade."

"The daughter of that man?" Nunoura said, turning back in surprise.

As if he'd been waiting for his moment, Henry puffed out his chest and adopted an imperious tone. "Yes, Anju is my daughter. If you have anything negative to say about her, by all means, let me hear it."

"Um . . . I didn't mean . . ."

"Hm?" Henry growled.

Nunoura was completely intimidated.

Henry looked like he had a few more choice words for the man, but Karin tugged at this sleeve.

"That's enough!" she hissed. "Let's go home, Papa."

"If you say so."

Nunoura and the others fled into the school the moment Henry turned away.

Karin and Henry walked down the dark streets together. When they were a safe distance from the gates, Karin finally voiced the question she'd been holding back for so long: "Papa, what really happened? The peeping Tom Mr. Kijima described sounds a lot like you."

"Oh," Henry replied in a cheery tone. "I was peering through the windows and accidentally made eye contact with that woman."

"Papa! How could you? Looking at kids changing!"

Henry darkened. "That wasn't me! That was an hour ago—well before sunset!"

"Oh, right." Karin felt small.

"I just got here. How could you accuse me of looking in the changing rooms?"

"Why did you come here, though?"

"I wanted to see what kind of man Mr. Kijima really is. I flew here the moment the sun set. I hid behind a large kite so nobody would see me."

People always were finding abandoned kites all over the city.

"But that horrible woman with the glasses saw me," Henry said. "She screamed so loudly that a few other teachers caught a glimpse of me, as well."

"So you really didn't peek into the changing rooms?"

"Of course not! The head of the honorable Maaka family reduced to charges of voyeurism? It's an insult to my name! May the heavens smite the real culprit!"

"Please, don't shout! What if someone hears you?"

"Harrumph! At any rate, there was far too much commotion to get a good sense of Mr. Kijima. I hid on the roof of the school waiting for it to get dark enough to go home under cover. Then, I saw him make you cry. Oh! I had forgotten about that. What did he say to you? How dare he make my daughter cry!"

Henry welled up into a fresh rage, but Karin interceded before he turned to go back to the school.

"He didn't make me cry! He was worried that I wasn't feeling well, and then I remembered what happened at work and started crying. He was trying to cheer me up!"

"So something happened at work? Was someone mean to you? Who?"

Karin hesitated. She couldn't tell her father any more than this without causing trouble for Kenta. "It was nothing. Please, don't worry. And it wasn't Mr. Kijima's fault."

Henry stroked his beard in thought. "Well," he said at last. "He can't be all bad. He defended Anju."

"Are you sure you've never met him before? He seems to have traumatic memories of a man in a black cape. At the amusement park yesterday, he freaked out at the site of a man dressed up like a vampire. He says he doesn't remember why. Do you know anything?"

"How would I know? He was a mere child fifteen years ago. Maybe if you had a photo to jog my memory—but looking at him now doesn't ring any bells."

"Yeah."

"Are you okay, Karin? You really don't seem well. I'm worried."

"Nah, I'm fine," she said, although she didn't feel fine at all.

Why does it hurt so much?

A few minutes before, Hidemi had noticed how depressed Karin was and had been so nice in response. And yesterday, he had cleaned up all the blood she'd lost without a complaint.

Her father loved her so much that he almost had gone berserk when he'd heard she'd been assaulted on the train. She had a sister who always found time to give her advice. And at school, she had Maki, who had been her best friend since first grade.

All Kenta had said was that he didn't care whom she dated. It wasn't like they weren't still friends. She'd lost nothing, so what was this weight in her chest? It was as if someone had filled her with sand.

Why? Karin asked the question again and again, but she had no answer. The streetlights around her were blurry through her tears.

The bat watching Henry and Karin from above relayed everything it saw directly into Anju's mind.

She had gone to the school that evening so that her bats could watch Hidemi, but now she had the information she'd been after.

"Chills when he met Papa. Hidemi Kijima."

Anju terminated the flow of information and began mulling over things. She sat on her bed, surrounded by dolls.

"What is it, Anju?" Boogie asked.

"Do you remember what Karin said? Mr. Kijima told her his heart beat faster when he was around her. When he's near Papa or me, the reaction is stronger yet. I think he must be extremely sensitive to inhuman things like vampires and ghosts."

"He said he's never seen anything like that, though."

"Precisely. He instinctively avoids them because he's so sensitive. Obviously, it's never occurred to him that vampires might be living among humans—but at the pool, he avoided looking at me. The aura of unhappiness Karin can feel from him might be connected to that sensitivity."

"You don't think it's about the black cape." Boogie's mouth flapped open and closed of its own accord.

"Right. However, this means we have a problem. Karin thinks Mr. Kijima's unhappiness has something to do with Papa. I agree. Judging from his age at the time, there's no way Papa would have drunk from him. But maybe he saw something he shouldn't have and had his memory erased as a result. The terror of that moment could be responsible for everything."

"So what?"

Anju looked depressed. "If vampires make Mr. Kijima unhappy, and he recovers his memories, then he'll hate all vampires and become our enemy."

"The first to strike usually wins," Boogie pointed out. "Erase all his memories. Empty his mind."

"We can't do that. His family runs a big hospital in Osaka, right? If he gets amnesia, his family will take him in and try to cure him. That could mean trouble for us."

"So, what do we do—talk to your parents?"

"It's still too soon," Anju fretted. "This is all pure speculation. And anyway, that time Mr. Kijima got so angry at school . . . that was about a prank some of the older kids pulled, nothing to do with vampires or capes. There must be another element to his unhappiness."

Anju cast her eyes to the ground, a rare sheen of regret in her eyes. Her long eyelashes formed delicate shadows on her cheeks. "Karin thinks he's a good man. I'm the one who pushed her closer to him. We need a very good reason to pull her away again, without hurting her."

# CHIBI VAMPIRE AND THE LINGERING EMOTIONS

Come on up! Chukka Banpaku, open until the end of August! Try them while you have the chance!"

Karin was back in the Chinese dress the next day, holding a tray of gyoza at the entrance to Amusement Square.

"Free samples! This week only! Try for yourself and taste the difference!"

She shot a look at the orange sky in the west, trying to guess the time. She would finish handing out samples at seven, which probably meant another hour of work. She'd been on her feet all day, and her legs were getting tired.

"Karin," a familiar voice called up from beneath Karin.

"Anju? What are you doing here?"

"Joanna asked me to buy her a new accessory, so we came shopping." Anju clutched a girl doll in the hand usually reserved for Boogie. Her other hand positioned an open parasol between herself and the sun.

"Oh," Karin said, backing a step away. She didn't care for this doll any more than she did Boogie. It had big rolls of hair and was dressed like a princess, but something about the way its eyes didn't line up made it terrifying.

"You've been here all day?" Anju asked.

"Yeah. I'll be done in about an hour."

"Has Mr. Kijima called you?"

Karin blinked. It wasn't like Anju to ask about things like that. Karin was convinced her little sister paid scant attention to the lives of other people. "No, why?"

"There's something I want to ask him. Will you let me know if you see him again?"

"Sure. What is it?"

Anju frowned. "Someone's watching us."

The sidewalk outside Amusement Square was packed. People stood talking on their cell phones, jostling packages, chatting with friends. There was no way to tell who was looking at them.

"Never mind," Anju decided. "Strange men often stare at me—one called out to me at school yesterday."

"That sounds dangerous!"

"I'm fine. Do you think anything actually could happen?"

Anju had a point. No ordinary human could harm her, not even a gun-toting yakuza.

"Goodbye," she said simply, fading into the crowd.

Karin turned her attention back to work.

"Free samples! Taste the difference for yourself! We have Eijirou's fried gyoza and Tenshinbou Dragon's steamed gyoza!"

A steady stream of hands reached out and plucked gyoza from her tray. It was nearing dinnertime, and the smell of garlic was making people hungry.

Karin headed back inside about twenty minutes later: When a customer fumbled his gyoza grab, he'd left a big grease stain on Karin's apron. Cleanliness was vital in food service; Karin couldn't pass out samples in a dirty apron.

"Out of samples!" she sang as she handed the empty tray to an Eijirou staff member. "I'll need another batch once I've changed aprons."

Karin was just about to push open the door to the employee's area when an older voice called out.

"Hey, you there!"

Karin turned around to discover a well-built man standing behind her. His face was etched with age, sandwiched between a thick mop of hair and a shiny suit. He looked familiar.

"Karin Maaka, isn't it? Anju's sister?"

It was the man who had spoken rudely about Anju the previous day, outside Aoba Elementary.

"Um . . . You're the chairman of the education board, right?" Karin ventured.

"You remember? You must be Anju Maaka's sister, after all," Nunoura frowned.

Karin nodded.

"My name is Nunoura. Did you hear about the incident at the school yesterday? The peeping Tom?"

"Yes," Karin answered. "Kijima-sensei told me."

"Kijima? Oh, the substitute. Why would he tell you?"

"We see each other around sometimes. I ran into him yesterday when he was out looking for the peeping Tom, and he asked if I'd seen anyone suspicious." She wondered why Nunoura seemed so intense. Maybe he was used to bossing people around.

Nunoura looked grave. "We found a major clue to the prowler's identity," he said with a low voice. "I fear your sister is his main target. We found several photographs taken of her through a telephoto lens."

"What?"

"It isn't enough information to contact the police, though; we have to be sure. Would you call your sister for me? You have a phone, right?"

"Yes," Karin said blankly.

"Don't tell anyone else—not even your parents. We can't risk rumors spreading while there's a chance this could be a misunderstanding. Bring your sister here alone."

Karin nodded. She knew how unsubstantiated rumors had harmed Hidemi, so Nunoura's words made perfect sense to her.

"My phone's in my locker. I'll be right back."

"Hurry," Nunoura intoned. "We must act before there are any more victims."

Karin ran to her locker and fished her handset out of an unruly pile of papers. It was the middle of the evening rush, so the employee areas were empty. Karin felt guilt about sending phone messages while everyone else was working hard; but if some creep were after her sister, how could she do anything else?

Nunoura hid in the shadow of the staircase, waiting for Karin to come out.

"What should I say to her?" Karin called out, holding up her phone.

The device rang suddenly.

"Hello? This is Karin . . ."

She answered it with the automatic response of a teen girl. She could see Nunoura frowning angrily in the shadows, but it was too late to hang up now. Karin could hear a cheery voice on the line.

"Hey, Karin! Do you have time to talk? It's Hidemi."

"Hidemi!" Karin blushed. She shouldn't have called him that in front of a board member. Trying to cover, she quickly added, "Perfect timing! You know that peeping Tom yesterday? Well, just now . . ."

Nunoura yanked the phone from her hand. He'd never been a very nice-looking man, but now anger made him very intimidating. Karin froze as Nunoura switched off the handset and jammed it in his pocket.

Then, he grabbed her wrist.

"What are you doing?" Karin struggled uselessly. "Ow! Let get of me!"

Nunoura scowled down at her. "Be quiet! I told you not to tell anyone!"

He pulled a small awl out of his pocket. The sharp metal point flowed into a thick handle. It was small enough to hide in a grown man's palm, but hefty enough to puncture a phone book.

Karin pulled away in fear, causing Nunoura to squeeze her wrist tighter. She could feel her bones grinding together.

Nunoura yanked Karin toward him and wrapped the hand holding the awl around her back. The top poked through her dress and pressed into her skin.

"Ow!"

"We can't do anything here. There are too many people. If you don't want to get hurt, come with me quietly. Any funny business, and I'll stab you. If we see anyone you know, tell them I'm your father, and you're taking me to the parking lot."

Nunoura began walking forward grimly.

Karin's mind raced. *What's going on? What does he want with me?*

She was completely confused. Terror left her skin covered in goose bumps. She could feel the sharp point of the awl pressed against her skin, destroying her attempts to think clearly. It wasn't as sharp as a needle;

but if Nunoura put any force behind it, she was sure it would hurt. Depending on where he stabbed her, she could even die.

Why does this always happen to me?

Karin already had been kidnapped by a serial rapist and a murderous nun this year alone.

"What do you want with me? Please, don't hurt me!" she pleaded, tears welling up.

Nunoura glanced down at her. "Don't get the wrong idea. I don't want you."

"Huh?"

"If you hadn't started to spill the beans, I'd have let you go safely. Kijima is that substitute teacher, right? That man always is getting in my way! At least he told me her name."

His features softened, his eyes focusing on an image in his mind's eye.

"I want your sister," he whispered.

"Anju!"

The sound of bells echoed through the house. The Maaka home telephone was a classic rotary dial unit, its ring equally old-fashioned. It clattered a dozen times before it stopped. A moment later, it was ringing anew.

Anju hopped off her bed in annoyance. Both her parents were out, which meant she had to stomp all the way down the hall to answer the phone herself. Normally, a ringing phone would most likely mean Karin had an emergency—but Karin would try reaching her sister by cell phone first. Anju had no idea who could be calling.

"Hello?"

"Anju, right? It's Mr. Kijima. Is your sister home?" He sounded very upset.

"No. She's working at the amusement center today. If you're in a hurry, you should call her cell."

"I did, but we got cut off. I don't think she hung up on me, though. And now, she's not answering her phone at all. I mean, knowing Karin, she probably dropped it in the river or something." Hidemi blurted everything in one frantic burst; then, he seemed to remember that he was talking to a student and slowed down.

"Excuse me," he said. "I know you don't know either. So, she's at work. Thanks."

"What are you going to do?"

"I'm supposed to meet a friend at seven. It's a little early, but I guess I'll swing by Amusement Square on the way and look for her. It's a short drive. I'm sure it's nothing—probably just dead batteries or something."

Anju knew he was lying. If he was going to all the trouble of looking for her, then he must be really worried. She decided it would be faster to look for Karin herself than to interrogate him.

"Okay. Goodbye, sensei."

Anju hung up and quickly moved to a window overlooking the garden, throwing it open.

"Find Karin. If she's in danger, find someone nearby who can help her. Go!" she ordered, and the branches rustled.

A moment later, all the bats that had been hanging from trees in the garden rushed into the air, covering up the purple sky before dispersing in all directions.

🦇

The town was getting dark, but it certainly wasn't getting quiet.

Kenta placed a cardboard box on the back of the truck before wiping a river of sweat off his brow. Heat radiated from the asphalt parking lot he crossed back and forth between the truck and the warehouse. He glanced down at his watch, mildly surprised to see it still working despite the damp on his arms. He was on his final delivery and estimated he'd be home by eight.

Kenta climbed back into the truck and pushed the box to the back. When he jumped down to head back to the warehouse, a voice called out from above.

"Yoo-hoo! Kenta Usui!"

Kenta nearly jumped out of his skin. Henry loomed above him, standing on top of the truck like a superhero. The yellow sodium lights of the parking lot threw an eerie pallor over his skin. Unlike his daughter, Henry was a full-blooded vampire. Kenta always grew nervous in his presence.

"What are you doing up there?" Kenta finally managed. "Get down before someone sees you. Hurry!"

"I was just flying over and saw you working hard. I thought I would offer some words of encouragement. Are you doing well?"

"Um, yeah, thanks . . ."

"By the way, about Karin . . ."

Kenta stiffened. The memory of Karin crying yesterday still stung like a needle in his heart. It wasn't the first time he'd seen his friend cry—in fact, tears came pretty easily to her—but it had been different this time: His own careless words had made her cry, and that was something he couldn't ever take back.

Kenta had no idea if Karin had told her father about the argument, but he knew Henry was extremely protective of his daughter. Any discussion starting with her name probably was not one that would finish quickly. He raised a hand, interrupting Henry: "I'm sorry, but I'm on the job right now. Let me go ask for a short break. If you don't mind waiting in the shadow of that truck, I'll join you in a minute."

Henry nodded.

Kenta raced back to the warehouse and told Sakata his stomach was acting up again. Kenta was usually a hard worker, which meant he could get away with a lot without anyone suspecting anything. He didn't like to lie, but his expression of guilt passed muster as dire need to go to the bathroom.

He slipped back behind the truck where Henry was waiting. There was no one else around, fortunately.

"So, about Karin?" he asked.

"Yes. I was wondering how she seemed to you today. How was she at school?"

"It's summer vacation," Kenta pointed out.

"Oh, right. Well, I'm asleep in my coffin all day. I never know if she's at school or work. Was she at Julian today?"

"Our shifts haven't lined up much lately. I've barely seen her."

And in that brief time their schedules had overlapped, Kenta had made her cry. Guilt bit into him again, and Kenta hung his head.

Henry failed to notice. The vampire thoughtfully stroked his beard. "I see. You may know that my daughter recently has befriended a teacher at Aoba Elementary. Mr. Kijima. She says he's just a friend, but she ran into him yesterday on her way home from work. They exchanged a few words, and she suddenly started crying."

"Crying?" Kenta gulped.

"Something apparently happened at work; when he tried to comfort her, she wound up crying instead. I spoke with him for a minute, and he didn't seem like a bad guy."

"I see . . ."

"So, when I saw you, I thought I'd ask how she seemed earlier in the day. I need to know whether Kijima is really a friend or not. If you didn't see her, though, I guess you can't help. I'll have to go back to my original plan and go to the school."

Kenta's pulse quickened. "You're going to ask him directly?"

"No, I'm going there on a different matter. Someone attempted to frame me, Henry Maaka, as a peeping Tom! How could I possibly forgive the real culprit?"

"You mean the one who peeked into the girls' changing room?"

"You know who it was!" Henry pounced on the implicit admission, eyes gleaming.

Kenta quickly shook his head. "No, but I was there when it happened. I was delivering something to the school and got accused of being the peeping Tom, too. A witness said the guy had black hair, though, so I was cleared."

"I have black hair, which is why they suspected me! Unpleasant business! Did you see anything that might help clear this up? Anything suspicious or strange?"

Kenta blinked. Hidemi had been so busy blaming him, and the belligerent female teacher so busy blaming Hidemi, that no one had grilled Kenta for clues. He himself had been too busy to remember. But he *had* been very close to the scene of the crime.

"Now that you mention it, there was a man who came to the bathroom but left without doing anything."

Henry frowned, interested.

Kenta racked his memory. "We were there delivering parts, but I had to use the bathroom by the auditorium. Someone came in from outside and stood there, not doing anything. He didn't even wash his hands, just went right back out. The bathroom is near the changing rooms where the peeping Tom was sighted."

"He may have fled to the bathroom and pretended to have been there the whole time. Did you get a good look at him?"

"All I could see was his back. He was well built and wore a dark suit. He had black hair."

"A dark suit . . . Could it be him?"

"Who?"

"They called him 'chairman,' so he must be from the Board of Education. He called Anju a 'problem child' because of her flashy clothes. Apparently, the board was inspecting the school yesterday. There were a lot of people—but it being summer, not many were wearing suits." Henry pulled himself to his full height. "Right! I'll have to find him!"

"Um, be careful how you . . . I mean, there were other people in dark suits, right?" Kenta hastily interjected. If Henry seriously questioned someone, they might well get so scared that they'd confess even if they weren't guilty. Kenta didn't want his vague description to get someone innocent locked up.

"True enough. I'll go to the elementary school and ask around. Thanks for the clue. Good luck at work."

Henry bounded away, leaping from rooftop to rooftop against the purple sky. His black cape flapped wildly. Kenta never had a chance of stopping him. However, judging from the lack of screams, nobody had seen Henry fly away. Kenta scratched his head in relief.

The thought of Karin still hung heavy in his chest, though.

Henry said Karin had burst into tears when Hidemi tried to comfort her. Kenta was sure it was his fault. Now he felt guiltier than he had before: He'd hurt Karin so badly that she'd cried, and Hidemi had been so nice it had made her cry again. Regardless of the rumors about Hidemi having harassed his students' mothers, if Hidemi could take that kind of attitude with Karin, he clearly was a better man than Kenta.

Kenta and Karin were just classmates. He'd agreed to keep her vampirism a secret out of friendship, but he wasn't her protector. Karin could see whomever she wanted. Hidemi had told Karin about the rumors himself, and Henry had a high opinion of him, as well. Kenta had been furious at being accused of peeping, but Hidemi even had apologized for that. Kenta resolved to apologize the next time he saw Hidemi.

Kenta told himself to stop making waves over nothing, and he had turned to head back to work when a black shadow swooped overhead.

"What?"

A large bat fluttered around his head, as if trying to attract his attention.

This had happened to him once before: He'd been looking for Karin during one of her nefarious disappearances when a lone bat had appeared. He'd followed it and eventually come across his own mother, lying by the side of the road. It had been clear the bat had been trying to lead him somewhere. Knowing the Maaka clan were vampires, it wasn't too hard to put the pieces together.

"What do you want?"

The bat screeched batty things at him.

"Has my mother fallen over again? Or did something happen to Karin?"

The bat merely fluttered its wings at the first question; at the second, it screeched again. Kenta decided that meant "yes." This bat seemed much more communicative than the last one.

"So, what can I do?"

The bat flew around his head, screeching several times as if to make him hurry. Something must have happened.

Sakata chose that moment to check up on things.

"Usui! What's going on over there! You must be done by now!"

Sakata had found him, a box in his hands.

"Yeah."

"Then hurry up and help."

"Sure!" Kenta called out. He turned to the bat. "Tell Mr. Kijima about Karin. I'm broke. I can't lose this job. And I made her cry . . ."

The last few words never made it to sound. He couldn't voice them.

Ignoring the bat, Kenta ran back toward the warehouse.

🦇

Nunoura had taken Karin to an underground parking garage.

They had passed several people on their way out of Amusement Square, but Karin had been unable to ask for help. Every time someone drew near, Nunoura would threaten her again. With the awl pressed against her back, she dared not resist.

Amusement Square didn't have its own garage, but there was a large underground parking structure for a mall nearby, with a passage linking the two facilities. The hallway was empty and grim despite the busy hour, as if Karin and Nunoura had hit some brief gap in the flow of people. Nunoura took advantage of the isolation to babble intently.

"She had a good side when she was young, but she grew more and more disrespectful. Who did she think was putting food on the table? Me! I did all the work. Every single woman gets snottier and uglier the older they get."

He kept his voice down despite the empty hallway; however, this seemed to intensify the fury behind his words. It sounded less as if he was talking to Karin and more like he was pouring out a rant he'd kept bottled up for years. He hurled abuse at his former wife, as well as his daughter, who'd opted to live with her after the divorce. Every now and then, he'd add a complaint about his daughter's distant youth.

Karin didn't want to hear any of it, but she had no choice. She couldn't work out what any of it had to do with Anju or herself.

Nunoura rambled for fifteen minutes straight, eventually running out of breath.

Karin decided to risk a question: "What does Anju . . ."

"You aren't like your sister. You talk too much. You have too many expressions. That's no good. Women shouldn't talk too much."

Nunoura irritably shook his head. Then, as if entranced, he murmured, "Your sister's face never changes, and she rarely speaks. She's like a living bisque doll, just like my Mary and Margaret. . . ."

Karin had heard the term "bisque doll" before; it was an old type of Western doll, of which Anju had several in her collection. They wore silk dresses and leather shoes, and they had glass eyes set into porcelain faces. They were supposed to be very beautiful. Her sister didn't keep them because of their beauty, though; she kept her dolls because their blonde hair would grow during the night. Was Nunoura a doll collector? It was a strange hobby for a middle-aged man, but it wasn't beyond the pale.

"I've hired children as models before," Nunoura resumed. "I've convinced them to come to my home for a little pocket money. It didn't work. They all started crying and screaming—or playing up to me, trying to make me like them. Anju, however . . ."

Karin instantly knew that dolls had not been enough for him, so Nunoura had begun collecting girls that *looked* like dolls, girls like her little sister.

Nunoura had been the one peeping into the girls' changing room at Aoba Elementary the day before. He had seen Anju and slipped away from the inspection tour on the assumption she was going swimming with the others. He had peeked into the changing room, but she wasn't there. When he learned her name, he looked up her address from the school files and tried to track her down at home. He was obsessed with her.

"The roads are so complicated near your house," he continued. "I got lost. I gave up—until this evening, when I saw her talking to you at Amusement Square. I knew the gods were on my side! Ha!"

"Why did you come after me instead of Anju?"

"I followed her, but she disappeared. So, I decided to use you to bring her to me. You started to say too much, though; anyone else wouldn't have mattered, but Kijima teaches at Aoba Elementary."

Karin knew that the chairman had to avoid people who worked at the school, or his lie about trying to catch the prowler would be uncovered. That's why Nunoura had stolen the phone and dragged Karin away.

The revelation made Karin relax slightly. Her captor was not after her, only her sister, and that made things easier. She knew Anju would be able to use her bats to knock him out instantly. Her sister's powers had yet to fully awaken, but she was a genius at controlling bats. Karin knew she was too old to rely on her kid sister, but there was no fighting it now.

Karin and Nunoura threaded their way through the parked cars to the back of the lot. Karin waited for another break in her captor's rant.

"Okay. So, all I have to do is call Anju?"

"Yes."

"Then, give me my phone back. I'll send her a text message."

4

"Idiot. We can't talk here. There's no telling when people will come by! We have to go somewhere a little more private."

Karin liked the sound of that. Anju obviously would use her bats to save them; if Henry or Carrera showed up, however, there definitely would be blood drawn. It would be better to go somewhere other humans couldn't see them.

"Okay," she said.

Nunoura scowled. "You're too obedient. You almost look happy."

"What? No!"

"I get it. With all the kidnappings in the news, your family came up with some sort of code, right? If you use a special word, they'll call the police? I can't let you do that."

"No, really! I was just going to tell her to come here."

"Oh, you will. I'll write the message for you, though. No, that's not enough . . . I need some leverage, so you don't try anything funny."

"Leverage?"

Nunoura thought for a minute.

"It's cliché," he said, "but I'll take a couple of pictures of you naked."

Karin blanched.

"I'll use a phone so I can send them to myself. If you cooperate, I'll destroy them. If you disobey me, I'll upload them to the Internet and put your name on them. I'm not interested in girls your age, but I imagine a lot of people would love to get their hands on them."

"No! I don't want to do that!"

"I don't want pictures of you, either. I prepared everything for Anju, not you!"

She wanted to tell Nunoura not to take the pictures if they upset him that much, but she didn't want to antagonize him further. "Please, don't make me do that!" she pleaded.

"Keep your voice down!"

A sharp point pressed against her side. The cold metal awl was still poking through her dress, pressing directly against her skin. Karin shivered.

She had relaxed when she thought Anju would be coming to save her; now, that chance had slipped away. She knew she couldn't let Nunoura take those pictures, but what could she do?

He led her to a large black sedan at the back of the parking lot. It was far from the elevators and entrances, so there were few cars nearby. The place was almost deserted.

Nunoura put the awl back in his pocket, still holding onto Karin's arm. He pulled out his keys and bent down to open the door.

For a moment, his attention shifted away from Karin.

She seized the moment and shook herself free of his grip. Karin ran as fast as she could, shrieking all the way. "Help! Somebody, help me!"

She was sure there would be a security guard near the entrance or at least some people driving in and out.

"Help!"

Her screams echoed in vain, provoking no response. She had no idea where the entrance was. Nunoura was right behind her, and he was in better shape. The sound of their footsteps bounced off the poured concrete walls.

Karin was out of breath before long, her chest ablaze. She never had been good at running.

"Help . . . me . . ."

Then, she heard the approaching sound of an engine over their footsteps. Headlights appeared around the next corner, coming quickly toward them. A car!

"Help! Help me, please! He's crazy!"

She leapt in front of the car and instantly was blinded by the headlights. The screech of brakes was deafening. Karin froze.

The small car jolted to a halt a few feet in front of her. Just as she allowed a sigh of relief to slip between her lips, though, steely fingers wrapped around her face, and the point of an awl pressed against the small of her back.

"Agree with everything I say or I'll run this straight through you," Nunoura hissed.

Karin could feel the point of the awl shaking against her skin. Her near escape, and the threat of outside intervention, had shaken her captor. His voice was tinged with panic. The slightest provocation was sure to set him off. Calm criminals were frightening— but a panicking, unpredictable criminal absolutely terrified her.

Nunoura called out to the driver, who had unrolled his window.

"Sorry! My daughter's involved with drugs and isn't herself. I'm taking her to the hospital, but she tried to get away from me. I do apologize." He turned toward Karin. "See? You're making trouble for everyone. Come with me."

The accusation of using drugs galled Karin, but she didn't dare speak up with the awl at her back. Shame brought tears to her eyes. If she said anything, he was sure to stab her. She had no choice but to follow him and move out of the car's way.

The car stayed put. A moment later, the driver's side door opened.

"Karin? Chairman Nunoura? What are you doing here? What do you mean that your daughter's on drugs?"

It was Hidemi Kijima, looking very confused.

Nunoura nearly jumped out of his skin. The spiel was useless. Hidemi knew them both, and the lie made it very obvious that something was going on. Nunoura was shaking so hard that the awl slipped out of his hand and fell to the ground.

Karin tried to pull free. "Help me, Hidemi! He's insane! He's the peeping Tom!"

"What?" Hidemi was so surprised that he stopped in his tracks.

The pause was all it took for Nunoura to recover from his shock. He pulled Karin into a full nelson and ordered her to shut up.

Karin ignored him, struggling frantically. "Let me go, you perverted freak!"

Then, she heard someone gasp. It was Hidemi. He wasn't moving to save her, though; instead, he stood rooted to the spot.

"You . . ." he croaked.

Karin's eyes widened.

Hidemi wasn't looking at her; his eyes were turned toward Nunoura and her, but they weren't focusing properly. He was looking at something that only he could see.

"Augh!" Karin shrieked. Her heart clenched so hard that her ribs pulled inward. A moment later, her heart was beating at a furious pace. Blood shot through her veins, threatening to tear through her artery walls.

My blood rush—from Hidemi! But nobody's wearing a black cape!

Karin gaped at him in horror. His black eyes had lost their usual cheery gleam, replaced by a deep loathing. She could hear his teeth grinding together. A snarl rumbled through his clenched jaw.

"I remember you now! Back then, you . . . a pervert like you . . ."

Nunoura trembled under the powerful rage that was directed at him. He shuddered, terrified. Karin wondered if he always had been weak, capable of bullying only weaker women and children.

All trace of his power gone, Nunoura shoved aside Karin and sprinted from the scene.

"Come back here!" Hidemi roared. Whatever had frozen him to the spot had vanished. He launched himself after Nunoura without sparing a glance at Karin, who laid sprawled on the ground.

Hidemi grabbed Nunoura by the shoulder, slamming his other fist into the man's face. As Nunoura staggered back, Hidemi kicked him in the stomach. Hidemi was smaller than the chairman, but he was very fast.

Karin pushed herself up on her elbows, staring at her rescuer in astonishment. He didn't notice.

"You . . . people like you . . . that day . . ."

There was no trace of the cheerful young man Karin knew. Nunoura had fallen to the floor, but Hidemi hoisted him up and set about pummeling his face.

"It was a twisted pervert like you that grabbed my sister and threw me in the river!"

Hidemi's voice was strained. Blazing eyes beamed from beneath his furrowed brow.

A horrifically powerful aura of unhappiness radiated from his body. Karin buckled from the sheer ferocity of his emotions, her blood pumping so quickly she could barely breathe. She collapsed to the ground, groaning.

She'd been with both Hidemi and Kenta yesterday, and her mental state had been all over the place. Karin had known her blood pressure was increasing, but she hadn't expected anything like this. She had to get away from Hidemi before she exploded.

She couldn't stand up, though. Scrambling frantically, she managed to hike herself high enough to rest against the car's tire. It was the best she could do. The kidnapping had exhausted every muscle in her body, but the blood rush was worse. Blood welled up inside of her faster than her veins could cope. She had expelled two days earlier, yet she was already at her limit again.

"Hidemi . . ." she groaned. All that came out was a faint whisper. It never penetrated his fury.

"Bastards like you!"

Nunoura had long since stopped trying to resist or fight back, but Hidemi pounded away like a man possessed. His obliviousness to Karin's presence terrified her.

Her whole body was on fire, and the blood rush would not stop. She'd never felt such a fierce swelling, and she tried to avoid thinking about the possibility that her heart might explode. Her body felt on the verge of combustion. Tears streamed down her face.

Inside her mind's eye spun the faces of her family . . . and of a tall, sullen-looking boy, who always protected her.

"Help . . ." she groaned, focusing her mind on his image.

Suddenly, she heard sneakers running toward them from around the corner.

"Karin? Is that you? What's going on?"

She knew that voice. Karin forced herself to respond. "Kenta! Save me!"

"Karin?"

The footsteps turned into a mad dash. Kenta, still in his Damien uniform, ran to Karin's side.

"Karin! What's going on? Did Kijima do something to you?"

"No . . . he saved me," she panted. "It was the chairman the whole time . . ."

Her voice trailed off as her vision blurred. Her failing eyesight didn't stop her from seeing a lone bat fly past her friend. She knew Anju must have sent it to lead Kenta to her.

The bat fluttered across the melee and landed on Hidemi's head. He shook violently, as if an electric current were passing through him. A moment later, he toppled to the ground. Anju had knocked him out successfully, but Karin couldn't focus beyond that.

"Karin! Are you hurt?"

Kenta helped her to her feet, but the feel of his warm hands on her back was too much to bear. Karin threw her arms around him and sobbed.

"I was so scared!"

"Karin?"

Her heart redoubled its pounding. It had completely slipped her mind that Kenta also set off her blood rush. She tried to pull away, but she was too weak to maintain her balance. She collapsed, burying her face in Kenta's chest.

Her heart beat faster yet.

"Augh!" She pushed herself away again.

Suddenly, she felt a presence at her back. She whirled around and saw Hidemi standing there, staring at Kenta. The bat hadn't knocked him out, after all; it merely cleared away his anger. He obviously had seen her throw herself into Kenta's arms, crying.

His expression faded from surprise to dejection.

"Oh," he said simply. "I knew it."

Hidemi shook his head, like a dog drying out. He looked up again and forced a smile. It made his heartbreak all the more obvious. "I can't say I didn't expect this."

"No, this was . . ."

Karin tried to shake her head, but the excess blood sloshing around her brain made her dizzy.

Kenta tried to say something, but Hidemi threw himself in motion before he could.

Behind him, Nunoura suddenly leapt to his feet.

Hidemi tackled him to the ground. "You aren't getting away that easily!"

"Let go! You're ruining everything!"

"You did that yourself, pervert!"

Nunoura had been completely overwhelmed during their first struggle, but he was larger than Hidemi—and now, much more desperate. He shoved aside Hidemi and tried to run again.

Kenta let go of Karin and ran toward the two men to lend a hand. Before he could reach them, however, Hidemi staggered awkwardly.

"I'll teach you a less—" Hidemi's voice suddenly cut off.

Something clattered to his feet. It was the awl, slick with blood.

Hidemi looked down at his side. His hands already were clamped against the wound. A red stain spread sickeningly across his shirt. Blood bubbled out between his fingers, dripping to the ground.

Karin knew Nunoura must have snatched the awl when the two men had fallen to the ground together. And this time, he had used it.

"No way . . ." Hidemi flashed a pained grin, as if trying to dismiss this turn of events as a joke. He held the expression for only a second before the light faded from his eyes, and he crumpled to the ground.

"Nooooooo!" Karin wailed.

Nunoura turned on his heel and fled.

"It wasn't me!" he shouted as he ran. "It wasn't my fault! I couldn't help it! It was self defense!"

Kenta watched him flee in horror. "Karin! Call an ambulance! I'll catch him!"

The chairman's cowardly plea seemed to have angered Kenta more than anything else. The boy raced after Nunoura before Karin could stop him. She limped over to Hidemi and folded to her knees.

"Hidemi, hang on! Please, hang on! I'll call an amb—Ah!"

Karin suddenly realized she didn't have a phone. Nonoura had crammed it in his pocket when he'd taken it from her.

"Wait here! I'll go get help!" Karin faltered, beset by another dizzy spell. Her pulse was getting faster and faster. She knew she'd never be able to go anywhere in her current state.

"You'll never make it in time . . ." Hidemi managed, offering a faint smile. "This is so uncool . . . just like the last time . . . when the man in the black coat grabbed my sister . . . I couldn't do anything . . . completely useless."

"Hidemi?"

"It's okay . . . I'm tired . . . so sleepy . . ." he said with a resigned voice.

The red pool around him continued to grow. Blood soaked the awl all the way to the handle. The full length of the blade had stabbed into his side. It must have ruptured an organ or a major artery.

"Wait! Hidemi! Hang on!" Karin sobbed.

He didn't answer.

Karin knew she had to get Hidemi to a hospital as soon as possible. However, she had reached her limit.

Shaking his shoulders was enough to drive her into a dizzy fit. She had no idea what to do. Tears in her eyes, she looked around her for a sign.

"Someone, anyone! Hidemi's dying! Please, help!"

Then, she heard the tap of footsteps behind her.

"If you shout too much, your veins will rupture." Anju stepped out from the shadow of the car with Boogie in her arms. She wore her usual black dress.

"Anju! You have a phone, right? Call an ambulance! Hidemi is dying!" Karin screamed, tears streaming down her cheeks.

Anju shook her head. "I don't want to call an ambulance on my phone. They keep records. And he's not going to last until an ambulance gets here at this rate."

"How could you . . ." Karin boiled over with rage. She reached over to slap her sister, but Anju was just out of reach.

"Don't panic, Karin. I said 'at this rate.'"

Karin was too emotionally drained to do more than stare.

"There is a way to save him."

The slight smile on Anju's pale face was far too chilly to belong to a child. Yet, it was beautiful.

"Stop!" Kenta yelled, running desperately after Nunoura.

They had bolted up the narrow staircase from the parking garage and were now running down a dimly lit alley.

Kenta didn't know exactly what was going on, but he was determined not to let Nunoura get away. He was absolutely sure it was the same man he'd seen in the bathroom at Aoba Elementary. That was enough for him. Nunoura was the peeping Tom from before—and for some reason, he had dragged Karin to the parking garage.

Kenta blamed himself for the stabbing. Hidemi presumably had been drawn to the scene by another bat. If he had left Damien immediately, maybe Kenta could have prevented the attack. He had spent far too long fretting about whether to follow the bat at all.

He knew instinctively that the bat had come to tell him Karin was in danger, but he stubbornly insisted it should ask Hidemi for help instead. It had taken ten more minutes of solid screeching for Kenta to change his mind.

Kenta felt inferior to Hidemi. He lived on a shoestring and was convinced Karin would have much more fun with the teacher. Hidemi was older, too, and therefore more reliable. If Kenta had followed the bat immediately, he and Hidemi might have been able to overpower Nunoura before he could've recovered the awl. Also, on a much more selfish note,

Kenta would've had the opportunity to apologize for spreading malicious rumors.

Nunoura raced through a vacant lot toward a side street. The fear of being caught lent wings to his feet, making him far faster than a man his age should be. Kenta didn't know the area as well as the chairman seemed to, and he was still recovering from his stomach problems. He barely was able to keep the distance between them constant.

Cleverly, Nunoura had stuck to deserted back roads, preventing Kenta from soliciting help from passersby. Warning bells up ahead signaled that they were bearing down on a small train crossing. The striped barriers swung down, but Nunoura darted under them.

Kenta unleashed a frustrated roar. By the time he reached the crossing, the train would have arrived.

Suddenly, Kenta heard the leathery flap of wings.

Kenta look up and saw a figure in a black cape passing overhead. It crossed the tracks and appeared to come down on the other side. The passing train prevented Kenta from seeing anything more. He paced in front of the crossing, trying to catch a glimpse through the train windows. He could hear screams and the impact of blows, but he could see nothing.

The train passed.

A tall man in a black cape stood on the other side of the tracks. Nunoura lay on the ground at his feet. Unable to wait for the railings to rise, Kenta pushed them up manually. He sprinted across the track and came face to face with the new arrival.

It was Henry.

"Kenta!" he barked. "What's going on? I saw you chasing this man. . . ."

"Yeah. He's the peeping Tom."

Henry stroked his goatee, immensely satisfied. "Aha! I went to Aoba and asked that dreadful woman about the dark suit. Only the chairman wore something similar that day. I sent my bats out to find him. And now that we have him, the charges against me are cleared! I feel so much better. I'll force him to write a confession before dropping him off at the police station. Say, aren't you supposed to be at work?"

Kenta recovered his breath. "Karin!"

Hidemi dreamed that he was walking along the street near his home with his sister Mika. The sun had just set, and the clouds were still tinged pink in the west.

He was fully aware that he was dreaming, but the reverie had no trace of the jarring incoherence that marked so many dreams. This was the memory he'd repressed for so long.

His sister was wearing a school uniform, with a headband in her hair. The sailor suit told Hidemi he was in kindergarten.

Hidemi couldn't remember why they were out so late on such a desolate street—but he knew what had happened because they were. The events had been buried deep in his mind for years; now, the memory was razor sharp. Everything had come flooding back to him when he'd seen Nunoura holding Karin.

A man in a long black coat had emerged from a side street and now stalked toward them. The newcomer was very tall, and he wore a hat low over his face to cover his eyes. Hidemi was too engrossed in conversation with his sister to register the stranger.

As the man passed them, he stepped sideways in front of Mika and flung open his coat.

Mika screamed and pulled away.

Hidemi was too late. He had no idea what was happening. He was surprised and frightened by his sister's sudden scream. He knew that the man in the coat presaged something terrifying.

Hidemi tried to run after his sister, but he became entangled with the man. They fell to the pavement.

The stranger bellowed something that was incomprehensible as he flung Hidemi into the roadside ditch. The muddy water was too shallow to prove a threat, but the shock of slamming into the concrete below made him more frightened.

"Mika!" he sobbed. He rose to his feet—only to find the stranger with his arms around her.

Mika, who was struggling to free herself from the man's grasp, never heard Hidemi calling her. She managed to strike a blow with her knee. The man crumpled.

Mika fled, leaving Hidemi behind.

"No! Don't leave me! Mika!"

Hidemi sat crying in the mud. He was too weak, too small, too powerless to act.

Then, he heard a sound like the flapping of a crow's wings. Goose bumps bloomed all over his body at the sound. Hidemi was wracked by an instinctive fear far beyond the terror he had felt at falling in the ditch.

A big man in a black cape flew down from the sky, landing on the man in the coat. The newcomer wrapped his arms around the first man, sinking long white fangs deep into his throat. Hidemi caught the scent of blood.

The man in the coat fell to the ground. His chest rose and fell with shallow breaths. The newcomer wiped his mouth. "Twisted pervert barely wet the throat. Good enough."

Hidemi ducked back down in the ditch.

The new man was more frightening than the one who'd pushed Hidemi into the mud. He'd done nothing to the boy—but the sight of him alone caused Hidemi's pulse to quicken and mouth to run dry. He experienced the primeval fear all humans feel in the presence of beings beyond their power.

The vampire noticed the child and frowned. He strode to the side of the ditch, hauling the boy to the road.

"You weren't meant to see that," the newcomer said, placing a palm on Hidemi's forehead. "I must erase your memories. You will forget the last few minutes. . . ."

"I remember now," Hidemi whispered.

The dream ended.

His fear of black capes had come from commingled memories of the flasher who'd attacked his sister and the vampire who had dispatched the pervert. Hidemi could remember the creature's face clearly now: It was Henry Maaka.

That didn't matter anymore, however. The hole in his side was very deep. Hidemi was more sickened by the feeling of blood spilling out of him than by the pain itself. The blood kept flowing, and he realized he was going to die. He couldn't bring himself to care.

Hidemi could hear someone screaming distantly: "He's dying!"

It was Karin. Her voice broke; she was crying.

Hidemi felt guilty now. Nobody wanted to watch someone die. Maybe there was no point in him worrying, though: Karin had Kenta. She might not have noticed the connection herself, but when Hidemi had seen her cling to Kenta, crying, he'd known. It was Kenta Usui she needed, not him.

Hidemi grimaced. He had lost so much blood that he couldn't open his eyes. His mind seemed so far away now. Karin was right next to him, but her voice seemed ghostly and detached.

"There is a way to save him," someone else said.

The voices continued, but he couldn't make out what they were saying. His ears didn't seem to be working as well as they once had. He tried to ask them to speak up, but he was too weak to say anything.

"I'll try it!" Karin said brightly. Her voice penetrated his haze.

Hidemi felt his upper body pulled upright by warm arms. Something round and resilient pressed against his chest. Even on the brink of death, Hidemi panicked.

He felt a sharp, sweet pain as something broke the skin of his neck.

Vampires. The entire Maaka clan was made up of vampires.

It didn't feel like anyone was drinking his blood, though—quite the opposite, in fact. A hot fluid poured from Karin's fangs, injecting into his blood vessels. Fresh energy poured into his system. At last, the fangs pulled out of his throat with the sickening feeling of an extracted needle. The hands around his back pulled away, and his head was placed on something soft.

Hidemi could hear a faint voice. "Don't you dare die! Never give up!"

He imagined he could feel tears falling on his face.

Hidemi tried to tell Karin not to cry, but he was still unable to talk. His eyelids still wouldn't open, but his hearing had recovered. He could hear footsteps running toward them.

"Karin! Karin, are you okay? What are you doing? Why is that man in your lap?"

A young voice interrupted the newcomer's tirade.

"Calm down, Papa. Hidemi was stabbed, and she's just finished injecting him with blood."

"Anju? You're here, too?"

"What are you doing here, Papa?"

"I was looking for the peeping Tom so I could clear my name. I ran into that boy Kenta, and he told me what happened. Honestly! Who would believe the chairman of the Board of Education would be a murderous peeping Tom? What a world. I knocked him out and dumped him in front of the police station; it wasn't too far to fly. By the way, isn't this Karin's cell phone?"

"You brought it back!"

"I saw it fall out of his suit pocket, and it looked familiar. Kenta is on his way here now. He's on foot, so he'll be another few minutes at least."

Anju confronted Henry. "Papa, take Karin and get out of here. Mr. Kijima has lost too much blood. Find Kenta on the way and tell him to stay away. We don't want anyone here when the ambulance arrives."

"What about you?"

"I'll leave as soon as I've erased his memories."

Karin looked over at Anju. "I thought you said you didn't want to use your phone to call for help?"

"I called while you were injecting him, using this." Anju produced a third handset. "I think it belongs to Mr. Kijima. I found it on the ground over there. Now, hurry up!"

Henry rose to his full height. "Okay. We'll leave things to you. Karin, hold on tight!"

The pair lifted into the air and floated out of the garage.

Hidemi watched them leave, trying in vain to call them back. He wanted an explanation, but he was too weak to speak. He tried to open his eyes once more. This time, he succeeded.

He could see Anju standing over him. She peered down at him with her characteristic lack of expression. A shiver ran down his spine.

Hidemi always had assumed his chills stemmed from Anju's extraordinary beauty, but now he realized he was wrong. His instincts really had been detecting her inhuman nature. He'd had the same reaction to Henry and—to a lesser extent—to Karin herself.

As if reading his mind, Anju whispered, "You are more sensitive than most humans. When you're near us, your nerves respond. That's why you react so badly to black clothes."

"Yeah," Hidemi croaked, his voice recovered. "My sister was assaulted by a flasher a long time ago. I was with her, but I was too young to do anything. Your father saved me. . . ."

The feelings he experienced every time he was near a vampire and his reactions to long black coats were wrapped up with his repressed childhood memories, bringing back the fear and powerlessness he'd experienced that day. The reaction was so powerful that it gave him a headache.

"You got so angry when the kids at school were flipping up each other's skirts," Anju said. "Your childhood experience makes you hate any hint of sexual harassment, right?"

"Probably."

"And that childhood terror got confused with your fear of vampires. I thought you would be a better ally for Karin than Kenta if you truly loved her. But you don't, do you? You mistook the fear you feel in the presence of vampires for love."

Hidemi knew she spoke the truth. His heart beat faster when he was with Karin. He realized it did the same thing when he was near Anju or Henry. But because he hadn't had reason to fear Karin, he'd misinterpreted the rumble in his stomach for butterflies. Or had he?

"I was serious about her," he said gravely. Hidemi knew they never would be anything more than friends. He didn't want it to be a mistake, though. Visions of her face flashed through his mind—memories of tears and laughter, the overreactions, the episode on the train . . .

"I really did love her."

Anju lowered her gaze.

"That makes it worse," she said. "Karin wouldn't be able to handle dating two men at once. Look how easily she bit you; that alone would make you a better partner in emergencies. However, it seems my sister will have no one but Kenta."

"Yeah. Sadly."

"Sadly? You don't hate her or our father?"

"How could I? They saved me."

Henry had erased Hidemi's memory for his own safety—but the elder vampire, who could have left the boy lying in the ditch, instead chose to pull young Hidemi up to the road. And it seemed as if Karin had bit him in order to save his life.

"My body causes problems for Karin. I guess it's a good thing she wasn't interested. Not that I'm exactly happy about it." Hidemi smiled weakly. He imagined this must be how a baker would feel upon discovering he was allergic to wheat.

He really had loved her.

Anju crouched down next to him, sighing. "I'm sorry, sensei. I need to erase the last half hour of your memories. I need you to forget that we're all vampires."

"Wait, please. I just now remembered, after fifteen long years."

Hidemi tried to shake his head, but he failed. He hadn't yet recovered enough to make any dramatic movements.

Anju's garnet eyes flashed down at him. "You must understand that we don't want anyone knowing about us. We may be vampires, but we don't do anything bad. It's true that we take blood, but only a little. And those stories about our victims becoming vampires are all nonsense. There are many people like you, who are instinctively afraid of us. If our existence became public knowledge, we would be run out of town."

She shivered suddenly, glancing toward the road. Boogie stirred in her arms.

"What is it?" the doll asked.

"Sirens. The ambulance will be here soon."

"We'd better run for it!"

Hidemi shot the girl a puzzled glance. "Why did you save me? Letting me die would have been the easiest way to keep me quiet."

"Did you want to die?" Anju responded quietly.

He thought about this. He'd been resigned to death when he was unconscious. He'd even thought perhaps it might be for the best. But . . .

The thought of Karin's whisper, her warm breath on her cheek . . . He didn't want her to cry any more.

"Karin would grieve if you died like this. Kenta would blame himself. If you don't care, I can always make the ambulance get lost and arrive too late."

"Hey!" Hidemi coughed awkwardly. "I do care! Of course I don't want to die!"

How could he give up after Karin cried like that? They might never be lovers, but the memory that the girl he loved had cried over him would mean something, however slight.

"I'm not going to die," he said firmly.

Anju nodded. "Then, wait for the ambulance. Karin injected you with blood, but the wound is still bleeding. The mental side of things is more important."

"I'll do my best, you heartless child."

"If you can waste your energy like that, you'll be fine. You're young and healthy. I'm going to erase your memories now."

"Okay. I would keep your secret even if I did remember, you know. Tell Karin 'thank you.'"

"I will. Goodbye, sensei."

Anju stood up and glanced at the ceiling. A bat swooped down, landing on Hidemi's head. The moment its wings blocked his vision, he fell unconscious.

The rays of the setting sun turned the linoleum floors a topaz color. The halls of the hospital seemed somehow brighter than during the day as Karin sauntered along them, clutching a bouquet of flowers.

It was one week later.

Hidemi Kijima had been taken to the hospital, and his life had been saved.

He had told the police he'd seen Nunoura trying to force a girl into a car in the parking garage, although things got hazy after that. The chairman had admitted to the stabbing, so everyone assumed Hidemi had lost his memories from shock.

Many questions remained: Who had called the ambulance? Who had beaten Nonoura bloody and left him in front of the police station? Henry had erased the chairman's memories, and the bats had erased the rest of the evidence. There was nothing to connect the Maakas to the case at all.

Karin's family had prevented her from visiting until things settled down, so this was the first time she'd been able to see him.

I knew Hidemi had seen Papa in the past, she thought as she wandered the corridors.

Seeing his face twisted in pain had caused Henry to remember him at last. The clan had discussed the situation, aware that Hidemi was especially adept at sensing vampires. His assault on Nunoura obviously had been driven by the commingling of his hatred of sexual offenders and his fear of vampires. Anju had erased his memories, and the family decided Karin could visit him in the hospital.

Karin found Hidemi's room and rapped on the door. "Come in!"

She pushed open the door and found herself in a private room with a large window. Hidemi was being treated well if the room was any indication. Karin spied a television, a washing board, and a refrigerator.

"Karin! You came!"

Hidemi looked well for someone in his condition. He was lying in bed with his head propped up on a pillow. A beautiful woman sat in a chair next to the bed. Their eyes matched, and Karin instinctively knew they were family.

Hidemi introduced them. "Mika, this is my friend, Karin Maaka. Karin, Mika is the younger of my older sisters. This hospital's very good at taking care of me, but she skipped out on work and came all the way here to look after me herself."

"Twit. I already had booked a hotel, so I'm staying the whole time. Be grateful."

"Ow! Don't hit the injured!"

"You were stabbed in the abdomen, not your head. You always were pigheaded. I told you you'd get stabbed one day, you stupid idiot."

"Come on!"

The filial bickering intimidated Karin. "Do you have a vase? I brought flowers. . . ."

"Oh, sorry!" Mika breezed. "You came all this way and we're ignoring you! A vase? Nope. I'll go see if I can find one. If you look after this fool for me, I'll bring us back some coffee, too."

Taking the flowers from Karin, she left the room.

Karin wondered if she was deliberately leaving them alone together. It was true that there was no empty vase in the room, although it was packed with bouquets more expensive than the one she had brought.

Karin sighed. "I'm glad you're okay," she said.

Hidemi noticed her taking in the flowers. "All the flashy ones are from people that know my dad. They saw my name on the news and spread the word. All sorts of people I don't know are stopping by to visit me, hoping to score points. I know I shouldn't complain— but I'm much happier to get real things like this." He indicated the dozens of origami cranes hanging from the headboard. An attached ribbon read "Aoba Elementary Fourth Grade Class" in childish handwriting.

Origami and hand-drawn cards littered a chest beside the bed.

"My dad got me this room, too. I couldn't afford a place this nice on my own. I keep trying to get him to let me move, but he won't listen. Of course, it gets kind of noisy when the students are visiting, so I guess it's good to have a private room."

Karin forgot her shame at her meager offering. She found a pink convolvulus in a tiny glass vase. "Is this from one of your kids, too?"

Hidemi blushed. "No. It's from your boyfriend."

"What? I don't have a boyfriend! Kenta is just a friend!" Karin's arms wind-milled wildly.

Hidemi broke into a grin. "Yet you knew exactly who I was talking about."

"But—"

"If you say so. Anyway, he came this afternoon. He said he wanted to apologize."

Kenta had felt guilty about buying into the malicious rumors he'd heard and passed on to Karin.

"I'd accused him of being a peeping Tom, so I guess we're even," Hidemi quipped. "But he said he couldn't forgive himself, anyway. He's an honest guy—but not too bright. He said he doesn't know what made him act like that, but I think you and I know. He'll figure it out when he gets a little older."

"Huh?" Karin was none the wiser.

"If you're in love with someone else, you really ought to tell people."

"I'm not! Really!"

"See? You're thinking of him, aren't you? It's so obvious. I guess that means I'm just a friend. When I said 'boyfriend,' my name never even entered your head, did it?" Hidemi tried to look nonplussed, but his sadness was evident.

Karin was torn between embarrassment and guilt. She hung her head.

"Sorry," she whispered.

"Nothing to apologize for. I knew there was a chance of that from the beginning. Forget it. I had fun being your friend. It was really good of you to go through all the trouble of visiting me like this." He flashed his teeth in a genuine smile.

A sharp rap on the door signaled a new arrival. Karin had expected to see Hidemi's sister return with a vase, but a different woman stood framed in the doorway. She had straight, severe hair and black-framed glasses. Karin had seen her before.

"Tsujiikawa-sensei!" Hidemi blurted. "Why?"

The new arrival took in the scene, sulking a little. "Why? I came to see how you're doing, of course. If I'm not interrupting . . ."

Karin leapt to her feet, crimson washing over her face. "Ah! No! I've got to get to work!"

She had about a half hour; however, since Hidemi had launched directly into the subject that concerned her most, it would be difficult to linger much longer.

"Okay. Take care," Hidemi said. "Say 'hi' to your boyfriend for me."

"He's not my boyfriend," Karin responded reflexively. She hid her head and tried to force the flush from her cheeks. "Anyway, get well soon. Goodbye."

"Thanks. You be well, too, Karin. Goodbye." Hidemi waved cheerfully.

Karin left the room, bowing at Hidemi's new guest. She wandered down to the first floor and joined Anju on one of the long couches nestled in the lobby.

"You should have come, too, Anju."

Anju closed the hardcover book she was reading. She stood up, fluffing her long skirt.

"I'm not in his class," she said. "It would look strange for me to go see him. I came all the way to the hospital, be happy with that. How was he?"

"Pretty good."

"I mean, did you find out how much he remembers? He was able to recover memories that had been erased years ago. Papa said we should be careful."

Karin had panicked the moment Hidemi had mentioned Kenta, so she'd forgotten to ask. Her sister had erased about a half hour's worth of memories, including the lifesaving bite. Hidemi shouldn't be able to recall her injecting him with blood, or her weeping embrace with Kenta.

A doubt nagged at the corner of her mind. She went back through their conversation: Hidemi had been convinced that she and Kenta were going out. He should only remember what he had known about them the night before the incident, and he had never seen them cling to each other before the attack. Karin wondered whether Hidemi still had his memories, after all.

Different people were harder to influence than others, and the teacher already had proven resistant to memory wipes. Anju had worked hard, but it might not have been enough in the end.

"What is it, Karin? Does he remember?"

Karin shook her head. "I think it's okay. We don't need to worry about him."

She was sure Hidemi would keep their secret if he still knew it. His smile had been genuine, and he hadn't said, "see you around," rather, "goodbye."

Anju studied Karin for a moment. "I agree. And I saw Tsujikawa-sensei with a big bouquet, so I think he's recovering from your rejection."

"What? Anju! How does that help him recover from heartbreak?"

Karin had seen Tsujikawa be mean to Hidemi, so she'd assumed they didn't like each other much.

"Remember when Papa said he got information about Nunoura from a woman at the school, and then drank from her? That was Tsujikawa."

"Oh, right. Mama was furious he hadn't brought any blood home for her. But drinking from someone wouldn't make them change their opinion of someone else."

"Don't you get it? Tsujikawa wasn't mean to Mr. Kijima because she hated him. He didn't seem to get it, either. I imagine he's in for quite a surprise." Anju smiled faintly, as if she knew every word being exchanged in the hospital room upstairs.

As Anju had imagined, Hidemi was astonished.

Tsujikawa Shizuka not only had come to visit him in the hospital, but she did so as if their previously antagonistic relationship was merely a figment of his imagination. Her prim clothing and hairstyle were the same, but her sideways glances and fluttering lashes made her seem far more feminine than before.

"I'm not interrupting anything, am I?"

"She's just a friend. Don't worry about her." Hidemi couldn't figure out why his guest was there. "Um . . ."

Tsujikawa hesitated, but then she seemed to make up her mind about something. She bowed her head. "I'm sorry. I must apologize to you. . . ."

"Huh?" Hidemi briefly wondered if he were the victim of a prank. Everyone seemed to be apologizing that afternoon, and sending Tsujikawa in could almost be considered a punch line.

"I was too fixated on stupid things like resumés and tenure. I was pointlessly proud. I'm sorry. I was just jealous because the students liked you so much, even though you seemed to spend all day joking around."

Hidemi didn't know how to take this. "Thanks?"

"Of course the children like you," Tsujikawa continued. "Your lessons make the subjects easy to understand. You're always cheerful, but not afraid to scold them when they need to be scolded. You're a much better teacher than I'll ever be."

"Thank you," Hidemi murmured. He had never in his wildest dreams believed someone could turn around so dramatically.

"I was mean to you because the children don't seem to like me at all. I took it out on you. I couldn't help myself. I'm really sorry. When I heard you were hurt, I was worried you might . . . I finally came to my senses. Mr. Kijima." She paused. "Hidemi."

Her voice faded so softly that Hidemi barely could hear her. Tsujikawa whispered something unbelievable, and then she abruptly thrust a bundle of sunflowers at him.

"Get well soon!" she blurted. She pressed a hand to her face and fled the room.

Mika returned a moment later.

"Who was that? Was she here for you, too? What happened to Karin?"

Hidemi regarded his sister. "Karin left a few minutes ago. That woman teaches at my school."

"Why's your face so red? Karin's that girl you were talking about last week, right? Have you been naughty?"

"I don't work that quickly! Anyway, Karin dumped me for another guy. Oh well."

"But she brought you flowers?"

"Tsujikawa brought these."

"Sunflowers? You know what those mean, right? 'I only have eyes for you.'"

"Huh?"

"You really ought to learn what different flowers mean. I guess it could be a coincidence. Only really anal people would worry about the meaning of flowers they bring to someone in the hospital. Give me those, I'll stick 'em in a vase . . ."

"Sure." Hidemi handed over the flowers. "Do you mind lowering down the bed? I'm sleepy."

Hidemi studied the ceiling after his sister left. He liked quiet girls. A domineering woman like Tsujikawa was the last thing he wanted. But the way she had acted earlier, the way she had squeaked out, "I love you . . ."

Hidemi realized she had worn pumps instead of the high heels she usually wore. It was as if she knew he was sensitive about his height and was trying to narrow the distance between them. He decided she might have an attractive side, after all. There was something appealing about the idea of a haughty woman letting him see her sweet side.

The initial shocked ebbed, and Hidemi began looking at things optimistically. There was no point in going back. Memories of clumsy Karin stung, but he knew time healed all things.

The streets were once more dimming with the onset of evening.

Karin ran desperately beneath the neon lights flickering into life. She had used leaving the hospital ahead of schedule as an excuse to go shopping, but now she was in serious danger of being late for work at Julian. She cut across the parking lot and reached the back door, opening it and running straight into Kenta.

"Ow!"

"Sorry!" she howled.

Kenta struggled with a bulging garbage bag.

They had seen each other briefly as they fled the scene last week, but she'd lost too much blood and was too weak to say much. She and Kenta had worked opposite shifts at the restaurant the rest of the week. Time hadn't been enough to put memories of crying in his arms out of Karin's thoughts.

She tried to slip past him.

"Karin, wait! We need to talk," Kenta said firmly. "I'm sorry."

"For what?"

"For buying into those rumors about Hidemi. I'm glad you didn't believe a word of them. I don't know what was wrong with me."

"Oh."

Then, she saw how serious he was, and she nodded furiously. "Don't worry about it! Hidemi didn't seem to mind. He said he admired your honesty. Anyway, I saw the flowers you gave him."

"Yeah. I didn't have any money, so I picked them off the side of the road. He seemed like a decent guy, face to face. I hope you two are happy together."

"What?" Karin wobbled slightly. "I'm probably never going to see him again!"

Kenta had been about to step outside to drop the garbage in the dumpster; Karin's words made him turn back.

Karin pressed on. "It turns out Hidemi is very sensitive to the presence of vampires. We give him headaches and make him nervous. So, today, we said goodbye. . . ."

She wasn't about to relay the way Hidemi had teased her about Kenta.

He blinked. "Are you okay with that? Never seeing him again?"

"There's nothing else we can do. He's nice. Ren could take a lesson from him. But . . ."

Karin thought about how much fun she'd had with Hidemi at Sky Land, how he'd saved her from the molester on the train, how she'd sprayed blood all over him, and how he'd waited beside her, anyway. His cheery farewell had been tinged by sadness.

She burst into tears.

"Karin?"

"He was so nice! He tried so hard to pretend his memories had been erased."

"Hey, don't cry here!"

"I can't help it! I couldn't do it. I couldn't be anything more than friends. I feel so sorry for him!" She grunted the words between huffs and sobs.

Kenta started to panic. "Stop crying! Please!"

A deep voice roared from the parking lot.

"You made my daughter cry!"

Karin and Kenta looked up in alarm, only to see Henry vaulting the bushes. He darted toward them, his black coat flapping like a living thing. His eyes were gleaming furnaces of rage. Henry bared his fangs.

"No!" Kenta nearly wet himself.

Karin's tears dried up instantly. She threw herself between her father and her friend. "Papa, stop! It isn't Kenta's fault! I was crying about something else!"

Henry looked from one to the other, suspiciously.

"I didn't do anything!" Kenta implored.

"I was crying about something else! Kenta was trying to make me feel better." Karin wiped her face with her sleeves, embarrassed by the spectacle she'd created.

"I see. In that case, I don't suppose either of you know of any destructive, vindictive liars? Your mother is hungry."

"No, I don't . . ."

"Sorry. I'd like to help, but . . ."

"Oh. Well, I must find one somewhere. Work hard tonight, Karin. Kenta, take care of her."

Tipping his hat to bid them farewell, Henry vanished into the darkness.

They both sighed.

"Your family is exhausting."

"Yeah," Karin murmured. "My sister insists they're happily married, though."

Her eyes met Kenta's, and her heart skipped a beat.

"Um . . . I didn't have time to say it earlier, but thanks for coming to save me."

"I didn't do anything. Hidemi saved you."

"He paid more attention to Nunoura than he did to me. I was so relieved when you showed up."

"Really?"

"Yeah. Thanks."

Their eyes met again. Suddenly embarrassed, Karin hung her head. Kenta said nothing.

Crickets chirped in the bushes, punctuating the silence that had settled over them. Karin imagined she could detect a slight sweetness in the air around her. She was incredibly happy they could talk normally again.

What now? Karin wracked her mind for something to say. So much for talking normally—her face was red, and she couldn't look directly at Kenta. She glanced back at the streetlights instead.

Streetlights?

Karin suddenly noticed it was dark out. She'd been running late, but she'd been standing around jabbering like an idiot for the last ten minutes.

"Gah!"

"Now what?"

"I'm late for work! Gotta go!"

Karin bolted through the back door.

She immediately tripped over something and went flying through the air.

"Aaaiiieee!"

The piercing shriek was followed by a huge crash that seemed to shake the entire restaurant.

The crickets stopped chirping, only resuming their chorus when nothing more happened. The pleasant sound signaled the end of summer.

A long distance call between Tokyo and Osaka:

"So, Kai-san. Volume three didn't have enough romantic comedy."

Seriously? How much more could I possibly squeeze in?

Naturally, I kept this thought to myself.

"The story was great, but there wasn't much about the relationship between Karin and Kenta. We need to get a little more excitement into the next volume, a little suspense. Will they fall in love or won't they?"

"Sure. I have Karin mixed up in a love triangle, taking a page from the romantic comedy classics. That should do the trick. First, I need to finish this manga script I'm doing for a different company . . ."

"Oh, of course! Plenty of time until the deadline."

"I've already written a scene where Karin gets molested on a train."

"What? Molested? Was that in the outline?"

"Yeah. She owes a new character for saving her life, so . . ."

"Hm. That might be a little much. One of our other books starts with a scene like that."

"I remember that. Don't worry. He touches her in a completely different place."

"That's not the problem! I don't want it to be too . . . vivid."

"Don't worry! It'll be over quickly. The new character saves her at the beginning of the book. It's just a little fan service, really."

"I don't think they want that."

"Really? It's so fun to be mean to cute girls!"

"Ignore your pet perversions and pump up the romantic tension."

"Are you upset about something?"

Okay, I may have imagined the entire conversation.

The book seems to have been published in the end, so I hope you enjoyed it.

Like I explain every time, this novel is based on Yuna Kagesaki's manga *Karin,* which runs in *Dragon Edge* [in Japan; in the USA, the manga is called *Chibi Vampire*].

But the books don't retell the same stories in the graphic novels—instead, these events take place in between the manga stories. This book takes place during the middle of volume four of the manga, after an August adventure told in the graphic novel but before the start of the second term.

This is the second of two books set during the summer, so the next one will be set in the fall. I swear! Autumnal. But the leads still will be in summer uniforms as it will be September. And I don't expect many scenes out of uniform. . . .

Oh, yeah—we already have plans for volume five. It should be out in the spring—so like this volume, totally out of season. Please, buy it anyway!

And there are secret plans still in the works, too!

Wrapping things up with the usual thanks:

To Yuna Kagesaki, who wrote the manga and illustrated this novel;

To my editor, and all the other editors at Fuji Mystery Bunko and *Dragon Edge,* and anyone involved with the production and sales of this novel;

And to all you readers—thank you from the bottom of my heart!

— Tohru Kai
January 2004
A stationary weather front hovered over us, refusing to move all afternoon.